"Robert Morgan has done it again! *The Promise* gives hope to all who are trying to make sense of the difficulties that come their way. God really does work all things together for good. And now we know how!"

Stan Buckley
Senior Pastor, First Baptist Church, Jackson, Mississippi

"Rob Morgan is a compelling communicator, and *The Promise* is a life-transforming message. I learned that my circumstances may not always be able to change, but my attitude can change and that makes all the difference in the world. This is one of those books that can reshape the way you look at your life's burdens."

Jim Burns, Ph.D.
President, HomeWord
Author, *Confident Parenting* and *Creating an Intimate Marriage*

"If you wish to be optimistic and hopeful, read this book. This book will take you to a deeper level of trust in our Lord Jesus. It is replete with Scripture, providing the reader with the strongest of all foundations on which to believe. If you wish to be encouraged, read this book. If you are asking yourself the question why, you should find your answer somewhere in this book. Rob's new book brings to life one of the greatest promises of the Bible: Romans 8:28. I enthusiastically endorse and recommend to you *The Promise!*"

Bob Fillingane
Owner, Bob's Books, Hattiesburg, Mississippi

"The first time I read one of Rob Morgan's book, I did not know him. After reading a few pages of his engaging writing style, I thought, *Who is this guy? I need to know him.* So I Googled his name and contacted him. His writing captures me both in content and style. The content is relevant. The style is captivating. Succinctly stated, read not only this book but anything else he writes."

Jim Garlow
Lead Pastor, Skyline Wesleyan Church, La Mesa, California

"Written with a pastor's heart and a preacher's clarity, *The Promise,* by Rob Morgan, shows how Romans 8:28, rather than just being a bumper sticker, contains foundational truths that will deepen our dependence on the God who 'works in all things for the good of those whom he has called.' Read, mark, and inwardly digest!"

Peter J. Grainger
Senior Pastor, Charlotte Baptist Chapel, Edinburgh, Scotland

"Reverend Rob Morgan has been singly blessed by the Spirit of God with extraordinary ability to exegete the Scriptures with clarity. He has served with distinction as a pastor for thirty years and is a popular speaker at Bible and leadership conferences around the world. But perhaps his greatest gift is as an author. Rob's doctrinally sound exegesis of Romans 8:28 is coupled with many heart-moving illustrations from his own life and that of others, which is sure to be an encouragement to the reader. Rob Morgan's keen mind and warm personality shine through in the pages of this book. He has a rare gift for communicating complex ideas in simple language."

M. A. Henderson
Executive Director Emeritus, The Gideons International

"For years Robert Morgan has inspired me with his pastoral insights and heartfelt storytelling. In *The Promise,* he celebrates the mystery and power of one of the Bible's most poignant verses. Thoughtful, inspiring, and comforting, this book will help Christians find hope and encouragement as they live out their part in God's glorious story."

Steven James
Award-winning author and storyteller

"Rob Morgan never disappoints me. I have read many of his books, and they all do what a good book should do: they make you think about life from a new and fresh perspective. *The Promise* is a brand-new treatment of an old and enduring verse! After you have finished reading this book, put it where you can find it. If you don't need it, someone you love will!"

Dr. David Jeremiah
Senior Pastor, Shadow Mountain Community Church
Founder, Turning Point Radio and Television

"Robert Morgan has done it again! With fresh prose, startling imagery, powerful quotations, and an avalanche of gripping stories—ancient and modern—Morgan encourages us to believe that, indeed, all those bad things that assault us are being engineered by an all-powerful God for our welfare. You won't want to put it down! But it's not just an exciting read. It's solid theology and thoroughly grounded in Scripture. No mater how submerged in intractable troubles, here you will find hope."

Robertson McQuilkin
President Emeritus, Columbia International University

"Robert Morgan is a gifted communicator who writes from the perspective of a caring pastor. His fresh exposition of Romans 8:28 in *The Promise* is filled with timely insights driven home by relevant illustrations that grip the heart and make the text come alive in practical ways. I thoroughly enjoyed the book and heartily recommend it to others."

Dr. Billy A. Melvin
Executive Director
National Association of Evangelicals, 1967–95

"In *The Promise* Rob Morgan has put walking shoes on Romans 8:28. He has then walked it through life situations, making application along the journey. With laser-point accuracy he has focused our attention where it should be—on *God* who works all things together for our good rather than on *things* that we too often dwell upon."

Rev. Jim Mullen
Managing Director, Church Ministries
Billy Graham Evangelistic Association

"First of all, Robert J. Morgan is one of my favorite authors! I daily read, *On This Day* and have been so impacted personally by the 'Red Sea Rules' that I share the principles wherever I go. So, it was with great anticipation, even heart palpitations, that I opened *The Promise* and began to read. For me, the 'God bumps' began with the preface and never stopped! My greatest criteria for a book is when I think, *I have to give this to so and so!* And that is exactly what happened with *The Promise.* I now know what all my friends are getting for Christmas! Rob's stories and applications are indelible 'spiritual markers' for me. In fact, I remember while he was preaching through this sermon series, a church member told me of the power of God in the teaching of this message. Now I 'get it'! What a relief in knowing, believing, and resting in the fact that 'All things DO work together for good!' Thank you, Rob, for reminding us all . . . my spirit just took a deep breath and I can face tomorrow."

Kay DeKalb Smith
Singer, Speaker, Comedian

PROMISE

HOW GOD WORKS

ALL THINGS

TOGETHER FOR GOOD

MORGAN

PUBLISHING GROUP

Nashville, Tennessee

Published by B & H Publishing Group
Nashville, Tennessee

In Bible verses at times the author italicizes words for emphasis.

FOR ELIJAH

Everything that happens to you is for your own good. If the waves roll against you, it only speeds your ship toward the port. If lightning and thunder comes, it clears the atmosphere and promotes your soul's health. You gain by loss, you grow healthy in sickness, you live by dying, and you are made rich in losses.

Could you ask for a better promise? It is better that all things should work for my good than all things should be as I would wish to have them. All things might work for my pleasure and yet might all work my ruin. If all things do not always please me, they will always benefit me.

This is the best promise of this life.

—Charles Haddon Spurgeon

Contents

CONTENTS

Ill that He blesses is our good,
And unblest good is ill;
And all is right that seems most wrong,
If it be His sweet will.
—F. W. Faber

Preface

I was soaking in the bathtub late on a Friday night when my wife shouted something from the bedroom. All I heard were the words "accident" and "trauma center." Our middle child was out in her car, and my nerves jerked into knots. Grabbing a towel, I ran into the bedroom as Katrina hung up the phone. It wasn't my child, but it *was* one of my "kids."

Emily Mynster, a sixteen-year-old from my church, had been airlifted to Vanderbilt Medical Center. I threw on some clothes and rushed to the hospital, where, as the family's minister, I joined them in the intensive care cubicle. It was the hardest night of my pastoral life. The person lying there looked only vaguely like Emily. Tubes and wires connected her body to machines and bags, her face was bruised and swollen, and medical personnel labored on both sides of the bed.

Her mother was holding her hand, trying to talk to her, but Emily had no response. Her father, a doctor, was in another room, consulting the surgeons. A few minutes later, he entered the cubicle, fell into my arms, and sobbed, "I've just seen the X-rays of Emily's head injuries. My little girl's not going to make it. Oh, Rob, this can't be happening. This is a dream. It's a dream."

The hospital lobby filled with teens and parents from our church who held a vigil through the night. For us in the ICU, it was harrowing to see the light gradually fade from Emily's face, like a flashlight whose batteries were slowly dying. About four in the morning, her father lifted a hand to heaven and began praying: "Lord, I'm Emily's earthly father, but I've come to the end of what I can do for her. I commit her into the hands of her heavenly Father. Please send Your angels to conduct her safely and swiftly home. Give her joy as she opens her eyes and sees Jesus. Thank You, oh, thank You for the years she was with us, for the joy she brought our home. Now may she bring joy to Your heavenly home, Lord, as we commit her into Your presence."

At that moment, I seemed to sense Emily's spirit slip from her body on the tenth floor of the Medical Center and, under the escort of a band of angels, wing her glorious flight into the presence of the Lord Jesus.

I left the hospital right before daybreak (and had a flat tire on the way home), and for the rest of the day, I tried to regain strength and prepare for Sunday's services. The next morning, our church gathered in grief. As I walked to the platform, I noticed that the shoulders of my suit were wet from the tears of various teenagers who had hugged me before the service began.

There was a lot of hugging that day.

I had prepared my sermon a month earlier as the first in a series of messages on the theme of God's providential oversight of our lives—the truth of Romans 8:28: All things work together for good to those who love God. Now I hesitated to preach on this subject at all, for it almost sounded glib amid the tears to declare, "All things work out for good." How easily our comforting precepts and powerful promises can become trite platitudes and superficial slogans if not presented wisely and empathetically.

But this promise from God is not trite nor is it trivial. It is truth—a truth we desperately needed at that moment. We live in a world of catastrophes and calamities, and none of us knows what we'll face from day to day. Without God's oversight, our futures are like a deck of cards scattering in the wind.

But Scripture teaches that we have a God who turns our problems inside out—*all* our perils and perplexities; none is excluded for those who are God-lovers, those called according to His purpose. He brings blessings out of burdens, and He knows how to wrangle gladness out of sadness. God's guarantee in Romans 8:28 can alter our moods, dissipate our discouragement, lessen the pangs of our grief, and usher confidence back into our hearts.

As I preached that Sunday, I sensed the presence of the Lord and I knew He had long ago foreordained both text and subject for that very moment. I thought of the words of A. W. Tozer: "To the child of God, there is no such thing as an accident. He travels an appointed way. . . . Accidents may indeed appear to befall him and misfortune stalk his way; but these evils will be so in appearance only and will seem evils only because we cannot read the secret script of God's hidden providence."[1]

Sitting sadly in the front pews were Emily's father, mother, sister, and boyfriend. After the service they embraced tearful well-wishers and drove home to find an army of friends gathered with food and fortitude. It was sometime during the afternoon that they happened to notice the Bible verse inscribed on that day's page of their desk calendar: *We know that all things work together for the good of those who love God: those who are called according to His purpose. Romans 8:28*

The Mynsters cherish that tattered calendar page to this day; it's one of their most prized possessions. And as they cherish the paper, they are resting in the promise it conveys.

---

1. A. W. Tozer, *We Travel an Appointed Way* (Camp Hill, PA: Christian Publications, 1988), 3–4.

We have to face it—bad things happen, and they happen with unpredictable frequency and varying levels of intensity. Some are mere inconveniences; others are life-shattering disasters. But as I learned afresh that Sunday, there is a promise—a single promise!—in the Bible that can meet every negative moment head-on, and given enough time, it will resolve our every problem.

It isn't that believers are unaffected by life's blows; it's simply that because of Romans 8:28 we have a different way of processing them. It isn't necessarily a simple or sudden route. Some problems are so tangled that only God can resolve them, and He detangles them at His own speed. Being an emotional person and a worrier, I've spent lots of time traveling the Triple-A highway of anger, anxiety, and anguish. Life is very hard and must be processed. But with the right signposts and mile markers, it can be handled from a perspective of hope, and we can emerge with obstinate optimism.

I'm not talking about abracadabra or hocus-pocus. God's promises are not magic wands that instantly make problems disappear like rabbits in an illusionist's hat. But we do have a God-given assurance that *every single circumstance* will sooner or later turn out well for those fully committed to Jesus Christ. That knowledge changes our attitude every day about every event in life—or it should.

That's the theme of this book, and it's so important I want to repeat it: *In Christ, we have an ironclad, unfailing, all-encompassing, God-given guarantee that every single circumstance in life will sooner or later turn out well for those committed to Him.*

This book is built on the thesis that the word *all* in Romans 8:28 is a huge word: "*All* things work together for the good. . . ." Nothing in your life can ever be outside those three letters: A.L.L. As a friend said to me, "*All* means all, and that's all *all* means!" There are no exceptions. That little word draws a circle that encloses every detail of life. Every tragedy. Every trial. Every teardrop. Every burden, however deep. Every problem, however complex. Every day, however cloudy. *All* things work together for good. That's why the Bible repeatedly says things like:

> Fret not.
> Rejoice always.
> Do not be anxious.
> In everything give thanks.
> Serve the Lord with gladness.
> Be strong and of good courage.
> Come before Him with thanksgiving.
> Rest in the Lord, and wait patiently on Him.
> Let not your hearts be troubled, neither let them be afraid.

Romans 8:28 is the promise that morphs us into resilient, cheerful people, whatever our temperament. It's God's darkroom in which negatives become positives. It's His situation-reversal machine in which heartaches are changed into hallelujahs. It is the foundation of hope and a fountainhead of confidence. Even our failures can become enriching and our sins can be redeemed. Even death itself becomes a blessing for the child of God.

So why stay depressed? Why mope around discouraged or moody? Sometimes we act as though God forgot to insert verse 28 into the eighth chapter of Romans. Well, try this experiment. Grab a Bible—you probably have one nearby—and open it to Romans 8 and see if somehow verse 28 was omitted from your version. My guess is you'll see it right there where it belongs, between verses 27 and 29.

Well, if it's in your Bible, it should be in your mind and heart.

The truth of Romans 8:28 can change the way you think, and it can provide a corresponding shift in your moods, emotions, and outlook. It can actually transform your personality and alter your circumstances in life. It can turn troubled souls into people of confidence and good cheer. It's the secret of resilience and irrepressible joy.

It's a promise with your name on it.

It meets the challenges you're facing right now.

It's the promise. It's God's guarantee.

Acknowledgments

Thank you, my friends and fellow members of the Donelson Fellowship, for allowing me to prepare and deliver this series of sermons and for giving me the freedom to convert them into literary form.

Thanks, Chris Ferebee, for being my friend and agent.

Thanks, Tom Walters, for being my friend and editor. And thanks to all your colleagues at B & H Publishing Group. They're earnest and excellent.

Thanks, Don and Debbie and Molly, for letting me tell your story in the opening of this book, and for what you mean to me. And thanks to my other friends who allowed me to share their stories here too.

Thanks and endless love to my wife, Katrina, who lives out Romans 8:28 each day and ministers in many ways to me and to others despite debilitating disease.

And thank You, dearest Lord, for giving me such a concise, concrete, and complete promise as Romans 8:28.

I've used it many times and haven't yet worn it out.

P.S. If you have your own Romans 8:28 story, I'd love to hear from you. We're considering a companion volume featuring stories from readers with personal testimonies and stories illustrating how all things work together for those who love the Lord. You can find an e-mail link on my Web site, www.robertjmorgan .com.

> Grace: *You know that everything happens for a reason.*
> Bruce: *See, that I don't need. That is a cliché. That is not helpful to me. "A bird in the hand is worth two in the bush"* . . . *I have no bird, I have no bush. God has taken my bird and my bush.*
> —from the movie *Bruce Almighty*

CHAPTER 1

Cheap Cliché or Precious Promise?

I'm writing these words shortly after returning from the graveside of a little boy named Samuel, an unborn child who mysteriously died in the womb days before delivery. I've known the extended family for many years; they joined my church not long after I came as pastor, nearly thirty years ago. Like any family, they've had their share of hardships, but this was an unusually heavy blow. Samuel's mother had expected to be nursing him in her arms today, but instead she buried him in the cold earth. A tiny coffin replaced the crib.

Samuel's grandmother, Kerry, has been a wonderful friend, and we've often shared prayer requests regarding similar burdens in our lives. As we walked among the graves back to our cars, I reached for her hand, and fighting back tears, she said to me, "I know that good will come from this, somehow, someway. God works all things together for good, and I'm just holding on to that promise."

Driving home, I mulled over those words. Everything happens for a reason. Good will come from this. It'll all work out in the end.

Mere clichés?

No, clichés are not helpful. Instead, these are soul-bracing realities that flow from a central truth of Scripture succinctly stated in Romans 8:28: "We know that all things work together for the good of those who love God: those who are called according to His purpose."

It's arguably the most powerful promise in the Bible. Clichés and platitudes are temporary bandages, but Romans 8:28 gives complete and ultimate healing to both our souls and our situations.

Human courage and internal fortitude take us only so far without a stronger wind to our backs. The French philosopher Voltaire once defined optimism as "the mania of maintaining that everything is well when we are wretched." Some people are blessed with an upbeat personality that allows them to view life through rose-colored glasses and "make the most of all that comes and the least of all that goes," as philosopher Sara Teasdale once put it. But even sunny-souled people can't ward off all the shadows, not for long, certainly not forever, not without a sure word from an omnipotent God.

Sooner or later, even the upbeat soul gets beat up by life.

We need a higher power, a deeper strength, a wider mercy, and a mightier word. We need a promise so broad in its scope that nothing is excluded and so infallible in its application that on its sheer word alone we are consoled, energized, vitalized, and innervated during life's toughest moments.

We need a heartening word during life's smaller battles, too, for we have our share of both. Unbalanced checkbooks. Speeding tickets. Cancer scares. High blood pressure. Car payments. Car wrecks. Gas prices. Foreclosures. Prodigal children. The death of a pet. Chronic pain. Stubborn addiction. Pharmacy bills. Broken arms. Broken marriages. Broken hearts. Broken heirlooms.

Problems come in all shapes, sizes, and levels of intensity. Some are mind-numbing and earth-shaking. Others are two-bit trifles; yet sometimes the smaller problems upset us more than the larger ones.

I've had my share of ups and downs in life; they aren't over yet. As long as we're breathing air, we're going to have good days and bad ones. And sometimes the bad ones are *very* bad. I know what it's like to be jolted awake at 2 a.m. with news you never wanted to hear. I know what it's like to face debilitating family illness and to encounter a string of disappointments. I've struggled with cycles of despondency and seasons of anguish. And like you, I've felt the sadness of standing by freshly dug graves.

Thankfully, I can say that in my experience thus far, the bad days have been exceptions rather than rules. But that's not always the case for everyone. Some people face a lifetime of adversity, and for most of us, the problems grow harder as we grow older.

During such times, we're swimmers drawn toward open water by powerful undertows of doubt. We brood. We fume. We feel sorry for ourselves as we battle waves of discouragement. We grieve and weep and sometimes feel we're drowning.

But consider this: What if you *knew* it would all turn out well, whatever you are facing? What if Romans 8:28 really were more than a cliché? What if it was a certainty, a Spirit-certified life preserver, an unsinkable objective truth, infinitely buoyant, able to keep your head above water even when your ship is going down?

What if it really worked? What if it *always* worked? What if there were no problems beyond its reach?

Would that make a difference to you? If you really believed it, would it shore up your spirits? Brace up your heart? Gird up your strength? Beef up your attitude? Put a bounce in your step? Put sparkle back into your eyes?

Romans 8:28 is all-inclusive, all-powerful, and always available. It is as omnipotent as the God who signed and sealed it. It's as loving as the Savior who died to unleash it. It can do anything God can do. It can touch any hurt and redeem any problem. It isn't a mere platitude but a divine promise. It isn't a goal but a guarantee. It isn't wishful thinking but a shaft of almighty providence that lands squarely on our pathway each day and every moment.

The Lord moves heaven and earth to keep this promise. He puts His eye to the microscope of providential oversight and scans the smallest details of our lives, working them into a tapestry of blessing, making sure that goodness and mercy follow us all our days. He turns problems inside out, transforming bad things to blessings and converting trials into triumphs. He alone knows how to bring Easters out of Good Fridays.

I thought of this recently as I read the autobiography of song-writer John W. Peterson, who has given us such wonderful hymns as "It Took a Miracle," "Heaven Came Down and Glory Filled My Soul," and "Surely Goodness and Mercy."

When John was a teenager, he had a remarkable singing voice and was in demand as a performer. His greatest aspiration was to be a successful vocalist. "Only in singing did I feel competent and confident," he wrote. "Here was at least one place where I could excel. I knew it, and I made the most of it."

John became known as "the singing farm boy." Local radio programs were featuring him, and his career was very promising. One summer, he found a job in a factory, working at a machine that made canvas wheat binders. It was a noisy factory, and John's machine was especially loud. He couldn't hear anything else; he couldn't even hear himself think. So he spent every day singing at the top of his lungs, making up melodies and pretending he was on stage.

Too late, he realized he was abusing his voice and ruining his vocal cords. There was nothing the doctors or speech thera-pists could do. "I put such a terrific strain on my faltering voice through overuse and inexperience," he wrote, "that I damaged it beyond repair. When I realized fully what had happened, that my voice would never again be beautiful, I suffered such an emotional shock that it took months before I recovered. Singing, I had had the power to thrill people, and suddenly it was all gone."

That's when Romans 8:28 kicked in.

All things—even a ruined voice—work together for good to those who love the Lord. Peterson later wrote, "But if that had not happened, I might never have developed as a writer. With my voice damaged, I turned more and more to writing and that talent was allowed to emerge and develop. What at first seemed a tragedy was used for good, and the course of my life began to take shape in a quite unexpected way."[1]

Peterson lost his ability to sing as beautifully as he wanted, but he has put a song in millions of other mouths and created a reservoir of music that will glorify God for generations to come.

Think of the problems, burdens, heartaches, and disappointments of your life. Is any one of them beyond the reach of Romans 8:28? Can there possibly be a trial that isn't covered by those three wonderful letters a–l–l?

No, not one.

For we know that every last detail of our lives works together for good to those who love the Lord and who are called according to His purpose.

That's God's guarantee for you and me and for all who love Him and are called according to His purpose.

---

1. John W. Peterson, *The Miracle Goes On* (Grand Rapids, MI: Zondervan, 1976), 71–72.

Ye fearful saints, fresh courage take;
The clouds ye so much dread
Are big with mercy and shall break
In blessings on your head.
—William Cowper

CHAPTER 2

Single Admission or Repeated Pledge?

Every time I stand up to preach at my church in Nashville, I'm dependent on a friendly young man named Wade Kilgore who looks sixteen (he's really twenty-five) with a shock of unruly hair, a bright smile, and a keen ear. He's largely invisible to the audience, but I'm very aware of his presence. I know he's somewhere in the rafters controlling my microphone.

The other day I asked him, "Wade, can you think of anything in your life that was very bad, but it turned out good?"

"You mean like the time the police burst into my house when I was ten?" he replied.

That piqued my interest.

"My dad was a drug dealer," he explained, "and my mother was an alcoholic. One night, the police rushed into our house, arrested my dad, and he later went to prison. My mom and little sister started screaming, and I knew I had to be strong. So as calmly as I could, I went into the back room and called my grandparents. They came and took my sister and me home with them, and they ended up raising us."

"What good came from that?" I asked.

"Well, one night shortly afterward, my grandparents dropped me off at a nearby church that was having vacation Bible school, and that evening I asked Jesus to be my Savior. A man in the church took an interest in me, and he would pick me up and take me to church. Pretty soon the church asked me to give a devotional thought every Sunday, but I had to stand on a stool behind the pulpit to do it.

"The man who brought me to church every Sunday also ran the soundboard during the worship service, and he let me help him. By age eleven, I was running the sound by myself. In that little church it amounted to little more than turning on the power at the beginning of the service and turning it off at the end. But I loved doing it.

"I've been doing it ever since. Here in Nashville, I work during the week for recording companies and sound studios, but it's what I do at church for the Lord that I most enjoy. This is the career and ministry God gave me, and none of it would have happened had it not been for that terrible night when I was ten."

Then he added, "Did I mention that Romans 8:28 is my life verse? All the bad things that happened to me during my childhood and teenager years have really turned out for my good. I can see it now."

Moved by his story, I thought to myself that maybe we should all make Romans 8:28 our life verse: All things work together for the good. . . .

And yet . . .

And yet several years ago, I distinctly remember worrying that I might wear that verse out. I might overuse it, as John W. Peterson overused his vocal cords. Could that verse be exhausted? As I pondered the problem, I realized that—like most fears—this one was illogical. If it's God's promise, then all the power of the Godhead stands behind it.

Since God is eternal, it is eternal. Since God is omnipresent, His promises are too. I'm never outside their range. Since God is all-powerful, His providence pervades every event of my life. Since He is infinite, His promise is perpetual. Since He is merciful, His promises embrace even my sins, and when confessed and nailed to His cross, even good can come from them. Good lessons. Good counsel for others. Good thanksgiving for His cleansing power. Good testimonies of His liberating love.

Perhaps my real fear was that I would overuse Romans 8:28 to the point of complacency. Ralph Waldo Emerson once observed that if the constellations appeared only once in a thousand years, imagine what an exciting event it would be. But because they're there every night, we barely give them a look.

Think of this: What if you could use Romans 8:28 only one time in your entire lifespan? What if it were like a voucher issued by the God of heaven, good for one occasion during the course of life? What if it were a coupon good for only one admittance? We'd put it in the lockbox and save it for the greatest tragedy of life.

But Romans 8:28 isn't limited to one application or to a few situations in life. It's constantly available and covers every contingency.

Furthermore, to make sure we don't "wear it out," our Lord has given it to us in several places in Scripture. If we look only a little bit, we find Romans 8:28 reworded, repeated, reiterated, and recapitulated in several other passages.

In other words, God has "dittoed" Romans 8:28 in the books of Genesis, Esther, Nehemiah, Isaiah, Philippians, Ephesians—and, really, in every other book of the Bible. It's apparently one of His favorite promises, as though He wrapped it up in nesting boxes, which we can open, one after another.

In this book, I'd like to show you some of those boxes—Romans 8:28 and its primary cross-references in the Bible.

But first, a warning. The truth of Romans 8:28 isn't an automatic promise. It's available *to everyone,* but it isn't merely *for anyone.* There are many-splendored strings attached. We must meet the conditions and exercise both obedience and faith in claiming the promises of Scripture regarding the "all things" of life.

It isn't a cheap promise, for Jesus had to literally endure Good Friday to give us Easter morning. He died to redeem us, and His redemption overflows from Calvary to transform our problems, pains, and life perplexities. It isn't a verse to be glibly quoted and carelessly slapped on life's uh-ohs like a disposable diaper.

When, however, we take Romans 8:28 as seriously as God does, we begin living on a perpetually higher plane. He gives peace amid perplexity and brings testimonies out of tragedy. He turns sadness to gladness and gives beauty for ashes. He rules and He overrules—and as Spurgeon said, "When we can't see His hand we can trace His heart."

Of course, like Wade Kilgore, we can often see the results only later. Life, someone said, is like the Hebrew language. It can only be read backward. Looking back, we see the hand of God with thanksgiving. Looking forward, we claim the promise of God by simple faith. We sink our fingertips into God's promise, adjust our thinking accordingly, bring our moods and emotions into line, and tackle each problem and period of life as though Romans 8:28 were an unfailing certainty, which it is!

After my wife and I were married, I was desperate for a job—especially after we learned a baby was on the way. I had no income, no insurance, and no prospects. We were making a little money working part time at nearby temp jobs. I had spent years training for the pastorate, yet twelve churches had turned me down in twelve months. Finally a church invited us to visit, and the congregation seemed enthusiastic about hiring us. We spent a wonderful weekend, and it appeared a perfect fit. Returning home, we told our friends of our good fortune and started thinking about our pending relocation.

Imagine my shock when the chairperson of the pulpit committee called with news that a majority of the church had voted for us to come, but the percentage of the vote was less than what the church's constitution demanded. We were "fired" before we were even hired.

It was one of my most painful disappointments, but looking back, I'm so thankful things worked as they did, for other doors—better doors—soon opened that set the direction of my life and career in a way that was only God-ordained. Katrina and I learned by experience the truth of the old adage "Disappointment is His-Appointment." It's a truth rooted in Romans 8:28.

If you haven't yet learned this verse, select one of the translations below and commit it to memory. That's a good first step to changing the way you're thinking about the "all things" of your life.

"We know that all things work together for the good of those who love God: those who are called according to His purpose." —HCSB

"And we know that all things work together for good to those who love God, to those who are the called according to His purpose." —NKJV

"And we know that in all things God works for the good of those who love him, who have been called according to his purpose." —NIV

"Yes, we know that all things go on working together for the good of those who keep on loving God, who are called in accordance with God's purpose." —Williams

"Moreover we know that to those who love God, who are called according to His plan, everything that happens fits into a pattern for good." —Phillips

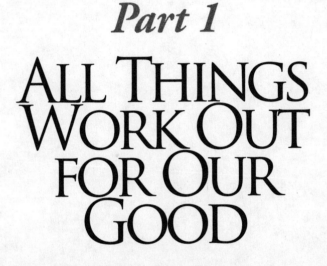

Part 1

ALL THINGS WORK OUT FOR OUR GOOD

We know that all things work together
for the good of those who love God:
those who are called according to His purpose.

ROMANS 8:28

All things work together for good
not by inherent force,
not by fate or chance,
but by divine control.
—Charles R. Erdman

CHAPTER 3

The Basis for Optimism

On August 24, 1890, Dr. John A. Broadus stood in the pulpit of the Woodward Avenue Baptist Church in Detroit and preached from the text of Romans 8:28. He was the president of Southern Seminary in Louisville, Kentucky, and had fewer than five years of life and ministry remaining.

"If you had your way," Broadus told his audience, "you would have no wants ungratified; life would be all pleasure; no rude winds should blow, and no chilling blasts should touch the cheek of those you love."

But life is complex, he explained, and hard times come. Yet we know from Romans 8:28 that all things—the pleasant, the sad, the helpful, and the severe—are working together for good to those who love God.

"We cannot fully understand now," he said, "but when we stand upon the heights of glory, we shall look back with joy on the things we have suffered, for we shall know then that our severest trials were a part of the 'all things' which worked together for eternal good."

Romans 8:28, he declared, is "the basis of true optimism."[1]

That assessment is both philosophically and theologically sound. The biblical word *hope* is akin to today's concept of *optimism,* and it should be one of the first things people notice about us. Peter told his readers to always be ready to give an answer to everyone who asks them for a reason for the hope within them (1 Pet. 3:15). A depressed, dejected, dispirited believer is a poor recommendation for the Christian faith. We're to be hopeful people—optimists—who have grasped the reality of Romans 8:28 and its guarantee of God's all-encompassing providence over the lives of His children.

This sets us apart from everyone else on earth.

Optimism is in short supply nowadays, and much of what is called optimism really isn't. If you ask philosophers about optimism, they'll point to the German thinker Gottfried Wilhelm Leibniz, who died in 1716 and is known as the philosopher of optimism. He theorized that our universe must be the best one God could possibly have made and therefore everything must be about as good as it can be.

That's not much of a basis for optimism, but that was the foundation for Leibniz's entire philosophical system.

The French skeptic Voltaire wasn't impressed. He ridiculed Leibniz in *Candide,* a novel in which the main character naively adopts the Leibniz-like optimism of his professor, Dr. Pangloss. But as Candide travels around the globe, believing it the best of all possible worlds, he is confronted with disaster after disaster— torture, war, earthquake, rape, inquisition, and slavery. Under the onslaught of reality, Candide's optimism crumbles.

In modern times, Dr. Martin Seligman of the University of Pennsylvania has done extensive research into the philosophy of

---

1. John A. Broadus, "All Things Work Together for Good," *Christian Herald,* vol. 21, no. 35, 28 August 1890.

optimism, and I've enjoyed his writings. His book *Learned Optimism* says that life inflicts the same setbacks on us all, but optimists weather the storms better than other people, being more resilient, healthier, and happier. Because of this, Seligman advocates learning to interpret life events as positively as possible. As we nurture an optimistic "explanatory style," it reduces depression, promotes better physical and mental health, and produces happier families and children.

But on what basis?

Interestingly, Seligman acknowledges that optimism, though necessary for mental health, is sometimes a "defense against reality." He wrote, "It's a disturbing idea, that depressed people see reality correctly while nondepressed people distort reality in a self-serving way. . . . There is considerable evidence that depressed people, though sadder, are wiser. . . ."[2]

In other words, though optimism may be a distortion of reality, it's nonetheless crucial to mental health.

Well, I want to be an optimist, but not at the expense of distorting reality or fooling myself. I want to be hopeful without being unreasonable or irrational. Good attitudes and healthy emotions must be based on right thinking, and I need a solid intellectual, philosophical, and theological basis for cheerfulness. I am not Candide, and I suspect you feel the same about yourself. We need an optimism that's grounded in realism, if there is such a thing.

Golden Words

There is such a thing, and the Bible states it in simple words that are timeless, truthful, and triumphant: "We know that all things work together for the good of those who love God: those who are called according to His purpose."

---

2. Martin E. P. Seligman, *Learned Optimism* (New York: Knopf, 1991), 108–9.

If the truth summarized in these twenty-three words is, in fact, the only basis of true optimism and the sole foundation for emotional health and positive mental attitudes, then we should study it as carefully as we can within its biblical context.[3]

Romans 8:28 isn't merely a snappy slogan to indiscriminately slap across life's hurts without a rational sequence of cause-and-effect reasoning. This verse is woven into the logic of the book of Romans like golden words crocheted into fine linen. It isn't merely 8:28; it's *Romans* 8:28, and we can't understand Romans 8:28 without knowledge of the book of Romans itself.

Romans is the greatest theological treatise ever written. It's the sixth book of the New Testament, containing sixteen enriching chapters that can rightly be called the spinning core of Scripture. More than any other book in the Bible, it systematizes and articulates what the gospel of Jesus Christ is all about.

Martin Luther wrote about it: "This letter is truly the most important piece in the New Testament. It is well worth a Christian's while not only to memorize it word for word but also to occupy himself with it daily, as though it were the daily bread of the soul. It is impossible to read or to meditate on this letter too much or too well."

William Tyndale, who gave his life to translate the New Testament into English, borrowed Luther's thoughts when he penned his own preface to Romans: "Forasmuch as this epistle is the principal and most excellent part of the New Testament, and

---

3. Years ago at Columbia Bible College, I was taught a Bible study principle that I've followed ever since. Every word in Scripture should be interpreted in the light of its sentence (verse), every verse studied in the light of its paragraph, every paragraph in the light of its chapter or section, every chapter in the light of its book, and every book in the light of the whole Bible. Only by prayerfully studying biblical passages in their context can we arrive at correct interpretations and appropriate applications.

the most pure . . . Gospel, and also a light and a way in unto the whole scripture, I think it (appropriate) for every Christian not only to know it by rote and without the book, but also to exercise himself therein evermore continually, as with the daily bread of the soul."

Background

This "most excellent" part of Scripture was written by Saul of Tarsus, the Jewish scholar and church hater who became Paul the apostle after his miraculous conversion to Christ on the Damascus Road. Following a period of seclusion and preparation, Paul began his missionary work in the Middle East and Asia Minor, then he ventured into Eastern Europe and Greece, preaching Christ and planting churches.

At the end of his third missionary tour, Paul headed back toward Jerusalem with plans for a fourth campaign to take the gospel westward into Spain. Since a church already existed in the capital city of Rome, Paul hoped the Christians there would help promote the undertaking.

In Acts 20, as Paul finished this third tour, he stopped on the outskirts of Corinth and spent three months in the villa of his friend Gaius. There he rested, recovered from his labors, and planned for the future. And there, probably in AD 56, he wrote the book of Romans (Acts 20:2–3; Rom. 16:23). He used the occasion to compose a written, systematized presentation of the doctrine of justification by faith. He wanted to ensure, should his enemies kill him, that his explanation of the gospel would be permanently preserved and propagated to the ends of the earth for all time. What better place to deposit such a treatise than in Rome itself, the center of the empire.

Justification is the act of God in which sinners, who are guilty before God and estranged from Him, are pronounced forgiven and declared just in God's sight through the merits of Jesus Christ. There are two sides to justification. On the one hand, our guilt is laid on Christ who bore it on the cross in our stead. On the other hand, His righteousness is imputed to us. The result is that when God sees Jesus on the cross, He sees our sin, but when He looks at the justified believer, He sees the righteousness of Christ. Think of it this way. What if you had debts totaling 20 million dollars, a nightmare of indebtedness that you could never overcome? Suppose a multibillionaire said, "I'll cover your debts; I'll wipe out all the red ink on your ledger." That in itself would be tremendous. But what if he also said, "Furthermore, I'll deposit 20 million dollars into your account, and more as needed"? That's a picture of justification. When we receive Christ as our Lord and Savior, the debt of sin is wiped off our books, and the righteousness of Christ is deposited to our account. We instantly go from being spiritually bankrupt to becoming eternally rich in Christ.

The theme of the book is stated in its prologue, Romans 1:1–17, especially in verses 16 and 17: "For I am not ashamed of the gospel, because it is God's power for salvation to everyone who believes, first to the Jew, and also to the Greek. For in it God's righteousness is revealed from faith to faith, just as it is written: 'The righteous will live by faith.'"

Launching into the body of the book, Paul asserts that we can never be justified—declared righteous in God's sight and thus qualified for eternal life—through our own efforts but only by trusting in the merits of Jesus Christ, perfect God and perfect man, who died and rose again for us. The first eight chapters of Romans lay this out in a logical way.[4]

That's why in our Bibles, the book of Romans is the first of all the Epistles. It comes immediately after the four Gospels and

4. The next three chapters—Romans 9–11 explain how this fits into God's plan for the Jewish people in light of the Old Testament promises. The remainder of the book, chapters 12–16, is practical in nature, describing the kind of daily life that should characterize those who have been justified by God's grace.

the book of Acts, which are historical in nature. Matthew, Mark, Luke, John, and Acts tell the story of Christ, the cross, and the church. The Epistles provide the theological explanation for these events, and the first eight chapters of Romans are foundational to all that follows. They are essential reading—the principal and most excellent part of the New Testament.

R.O.M.A.N.S.

We can understand the unfolding content of Romans by the very title of the book itself.

R—Ruin (1:18–3:20)

This section deals with the hopeless condition of humanity. We have all fallen short of God's holy character, reflected in the Old Testament Law and in the Ten Commandments. The human race has been ruined by sin and separated from its Creator, and we can never justify ourselves by trying to live a righteous life, for there is none righteous, no not one: "For no flesh will be justified in His sight by the works of the law" (3:20).

O—Offer (3:21–31)

God, in His infinite grace, offers us another way to be saved— not by keeping the law but by faith in Him who died for us: "But now, apart from the law, God's righteousness has been revealed . . . God's righteousness through faith in Jesus Christ, to all who believe. . . . For all have sinned and fall short of the glory of God. They are justified freely by His grace through the redemption that is in Christ Jesus. God presented Him as a propitiation through faith in His blood" (3:21–25a).

M—Model (4)

In chapter 4, Paul anticipated a question from his readers: "Is this a new doctrine you've come up with? Is this a new teaching,

Paul? Something you've thought up?" His answer: No, the principle of justification by grace through faith goes back to the first book of the Bible, back to the patriarch Abraham himself, the model for all those who are saved by grace through faith. "'Abraham believed God, and it was credited to him for righteousness.' ... Now 'it was credited to him' was not written for Abraham alone, but also for us. It will be credited to us who believe in Him who raised Jesus our Lord from the dead. He was delivered up for our trespasses and raised for our justification" (4:3, 23–25).

A—Access (5:1–11)

The first eleven verses of chapter 5 summarize the blessings and benefits we receive by being justified by grace. Justification gives us access to God's presence and to all the other privileges that accompany God's grace: "Therefore, since we have been declared righteous by faith, we have peace with God through our Lord Jesus Christ. Also through Him, we have obtained access by faith into this grace in which we stand, and we rejoice in the hope of the glory of God" (5:1–2).

N—New Adam (5:12–21)

As condemned sinners, our old forefather was Adam, whose sin contaminated the human bloodstream and infected us all with the toxins of a sinful nature. But now justified, we are children of the New Adam, the Lord Jesus Christ, and have inherited His righteous nature: "Since by the one man's trespass, death reigned through that one man, how much more will those who receive the overflow of grace and the gift of righteousness reign in life through the one man, Jesus Christ" (5:17).

S—Sanctification (6–8)

Though we should "reign in life," the vestiges of Adam's old nature still twitch within us and we need the supernatural aid of the

Holy Spirit to channel Christ's triumphant life through us. Sanctification is that process by which we are set apart for Christ and grow up in Him. Our old nature has died in Christ (chap. 6), but we still struggle with temptation and sin (chap. 7). The Holy Spirit is our great inner resource, making us more than conquerors (chap. 8).

Romans 8

Chapter 8 of Romans, then, is devoted to the victory that comes into the hearts of justified believers through the risen Christ by the indwelling Spirit. Because Jesus Himself lives in us and through us by the Holy Spirit, we enjoy in our own personalities His own purity, holiness, healthy spirits, and joyful attitudes.

Romans 8 is all about the Holy Spirit's work in our lives. In Romans 7, as Paul discussed our struggles with sin, the pronoun *I* occurs thirty-one times and the word *Spirit* only once. In Romans 8, as he talked about our victorious life, the word *Spirit* occurs nineteen times, and *I* only twice.

The Spirit reproduces the righteous life of the Lord Jesus Christ within us (vv. 1–10), guarantees our hope and future bodily resurrection (v. 11), leads us all our days from now till then (v. 14), assures our hearts of our eternal salvation (vv. 1–17), and sustains us during difficult times (vv. 18–25).

The discussion in Romans 8:18–25 of the Holy Spirit's help in difficult times provides the prelude to Romans 8:28. Though eager for heaven, we currently experience suffering in life. These present sufferings aren't worth comparing to the glory that will be revealed (v. 18), but they nevertheless make us groan. In fact, the whole creation is groaning (v. 22), and even justified believers groan amid life's troubles (v. 23).

"The sufferings of this present time are not worth comparing with the glory that is going to be revealed to us. . . . For we know that the whole creation has been groaning. . . . And not only that, but we ourselves who have the Spirit as the firstfruits—we also groan within ourselves" (8:18, 22a, 23a).

Verse 26, however, reveals an astounding truth: As we groan in suffering, the Holy Spirit groans in prayer. He does so on our behalf, interceding for us "with unspoken groanings."[5]

Think of it: Someone is praying for you!

I know from experience what it's like when others pray. Recently, I suffered a terrible blow when an associate on our church staff, a young man who in many ways was my best friend and a sort of son in the gospel to me, fell into sin. Because of the nature of the offense, I had to fire him on the spot. It was a deeply personal trauma, not only for him but also for me, and it struck as I was dealing with other personal and pastoral pressures.

For several days I felt as if a bomb had exploded in my life. I was unable to get my bearings, unable to think or function, unable to feel anything except overwhelming sadness and depression. Our church is filled with praying people, and I knew many were praying for me, but I felt no strength from it.

Then, late in the week, I took my journal to a coffee shop, found a table, and sat there in a state of numbness. I tried to express my feeling on paper but couldn't. Then in a way I can't explain, my spirits lifted, the burden lessened, my mind cleared, and a beam of hope pierced the clouds. At that moment, the tide turned, both in my attitude and in my ability to lead our church through the crisis. It felt as though the bottled-up prayers of many people had suddenly been released and had hit me like an invisible wave of grace.

I knew someone had been praying for me.

---

5. Later, in verse 34, we read that Jesus prays for us too: "Christ Jesus is the One who died, but even more, has been raised; He also is at the right hand of God and intercedes for us." As Moses was supported in Exodus 17:12 by the prayers of Aaron and Hur, one holding up his left hand and the other his right, so we're supported every moment of our lives by two divine prayer warriors, the Son and the Spirit, interceding for us before the very throne of God in heaven.

Now, looking back at it, I realize it wasn't only my friends and church members who were praying. I had a prayer partner in heaven, the Holy Spirit, pleading my needs before the Father's throne. So do you. The Holy Spirit intercedes for us with groanings too deep for words. It's part and parcel of our justification.[6]

But there's even more to it than that. Look at Romans 8:26 again: "The Spirit also joins to help in our weakness, because we do not know what to pray for as we should, but the Spirit Himself intercedes for us with unspoken groanings."

Weak Prayers

This verse implies we have many weaknesses when we try to pray. What weakness exists in your life of prayer? Maybe you're weak in your ability to concentrate, in the time you spend on your knees, or in your zeal and fervor. Does your mind drift? Is your heart lax and listless? Do you feel ineffective in your praying? Is your faith weak and spotty?

All those things are frequently true for me, and sometimes I pray for only a few moments when I should pray for an hour. I have many weaknesses in my prayer habits, and I suppose you do too.

But Paul was not talking about any of those weaknesses in verse 26. He was thinking of another weakness, a specific problem that perhaps you've never considered.

We often do not know *what* to pray for. We offer our prayer requests with limited knowledge. Of course, when we pray for things like a stronger faith, a more loving attitude, or for the Lord to quickly come, we can present *those* requests with total confidence that we're praying according to God's will, for His

---

6. Even the patriarch Job had a level of understanding about this in the Old Testament. In the midst of his suffering, he said, "Even now my witness is in heaven; my advocate is on high. My intercessor is my friend . . . On behalf of a human being he pleads with God as one pleads for a friend" (Job 16:19–21 TNIV).

Word endorses those things. But when we pray about specific circumstances in our lives, it's different. How do we know what's best when we can't predict the future? Perhaps the job we want so badly would be a disaster for us if we could see only five years into the future. Since we can't predict how events will unfold, we can't be sure how things will turn out or which things are really for our benefit.

There's an oft-told story—I first read it in a clipping years ago—that illustrates this. A wise old Chinese gentleman lived on the troubled Mongolian border. One day his favorite horse, a beautiful white mare, jumped the fence and was seized on the other side by the enemy. His friends came to comfort him. "We're so sorry about your horse," they said. "That's bad news."

"How do you know it's bad news?" he asked. "It might be good news."

A week later, the man looked out his window to see his mare returning at breakneck speed, and alongside her was a beautiful stallion. He put both horses into the enclosure, and his friends came to admire the new addition. "What a beautiful horse," they said. "That's good news."

"How do you know it's good news?" replied the man. "It might be bad news."

The next day, the man's only son decided to try riding the stallion. It threw him, and he landed painfully, breaking his leg. The friends made another visit, all of them sympathetic, saying, "We're so sorry about this. It's such bad news."

"How do you know it's bad news?" replied the man. "It might be good news."

Within a month, a terrible war broke out between China and Mongolia. The Chinese recruiters came through the area, pressing all the young men into the army. All of them perished—except for the man's son, who couldn't go off to war because of his broken leg.

"You see," said the gentleman. "The things you considered good were actually bad, and the things that seemed to be bad news were actually for our good."

We can't see into tomorrow, so we don't know how things will turn out. How do you know if it's best to buy the house you're considering? How do you know if your child should be accepted into a particular college? How do you know if you should make this investment or that one? What about that big trip you're planning? The healing you desire? The relationship you crave? The academic program you're considering?

Benjamin Disraeli, the British prime minister of an earlier era, understood this. "What we anticipate seldom occurs," he quipped. "What we least expected generally happens; and time can only prove which is most for our advantage."[7]

Since we don't know which things will turn out advantageously, we should do as James 4:15 advises and pray, "If the Lord wills." When I pray for specific things, I try to say, "Lord, if it is Your will, please do this or that," or "If it seems good to You, grant this or that." Even if I don't say those exact words, I try to pray with a yielded attitude because I seldom know what is ultimately best in any particular set of circumstances.

The Holy Spirit, however, being God, is omniscient, so He knows the future as well as the past. He sees every cause and effect, every chain reaction and ripple effect, every domino from now to eternity. He's an infinite chess player who perceives every sequential consequence of every move from now into the boundless future. As a result, He knows exactly how to pray for us, what to request on our behalf, and what dangers to pray against. Being God, He also fully knows God's ultimate and infinite will for our lives.

---

7. Hesketh Pearson, *Dizzy: The Life and Personality of Benjamin Disraeli* (Grosset and Dunlap, 1951), 55.

Hence, knowing the future perfectly and knowing God's will totally, He can pray specifically for every detail of our lives.

Here's something else. According to this verse, He does so with great fervor, with deepest feelings of love on our behalf, with groanings that go beyond words: "The Spirit also joins to help in our weakness, because we do not know what to pray for as we should, but the Spirit Himself intercedes for us with unspoken groanings."

That's Romans 8:26.

The result, declared in Romans 8:27, is that the heavenly Father answers these earnest prayers offered by the Spirit on our behalf. "He who searches the hearts knows the Spirit's mind-set, because He intercedes for the saints according to the will of God."

And the result of that is . . .

Romans 8:28—all things work out for good in the lives of those for whom the Spirit is praying, for those who love God and are called according to His purpose.

The Holy Spirit helps our weakness	
We do not know the future.	We do not know what to pray for.

The Spirit Knows the Future	The Spirit Knows God's Will

The Holy Spirit prays for us with earnest groans

All things work together for good

Romans 8:28, then, isn't a miscellaneous motto, an isolated promise, or a random verse. It is imbedded into the book of Romans like a tree whose roots are coiled around underground boulders. It flows out of the justification that Christ purchased on the cross, and it occurs because of the powerful and omniscient intercession of the Holy Spirit.

When you look behind the curtain of Romans 8:28, you see the machinery of Trinitarian involvement. The whole Godhead is involved in this—Father, Son, and Holy Ghost. It is a promise signed and sealed by each member of the Trinity.

- God the Son guarantees Romans 8:28 by His blood *purchase* of justification. It's part of His glorious redemption. Precisely as He redeems our souls from death, He redeems our sins, mistakes, situations, and sufferings for our good.
- God the Spirit guarantees Romans 8:28 by His earnest *prayers* on our behalf as He fervently intercedes for us with omniscient wisdom and according to the Father's will.
- God the Father guarantees Romans 8:28 by His omnipotent *providence* that rules and overrules every situation in our lives. Responding to the blood of Christ and the prayers of the Spirit, He providentially works all things for our benefit and His glory.

And that's why Romans 8:28 is the basis for true optimism.

CHAPTER 4

We Know

We know that all things work together
for the good of those who love God:
those who are called according to His purpose.

Several years ago as I preached from Romans 8:28, a member of my church told me her story. In the winter of 1988, Janice, her husband, and three teenage sons were living in North Dakota on a struggling dairy farm. The temperatures were well below zero, and they were crammed into a trailer with drafty windows and a leaking roof.

On January 8, the trailer burned down. "That's when I learned the truth of Romans 8:28," Janice told me as she related all the good things that came from this calamity. She was at work in a nearby town when the news reached her. Her first response was thankfulness, for all five family members were alive.

Rushing to the scene, she realized there was nothing to salvage. All that remained were charred and twisted steel support beams, smoldering ashes, and the blackened carcasses of her washer and dryer. The family moved into a relative's old farmhouse, which was spacious and comfortable.

"When our trailer burned down and we moved in with my mother-in-law," she told me, "I couldn't sleep that first night, so I went to the kitchen and with tears in my eyes saw that my mother-in-law had left her Bible on the kitchen table. I flipped it open at random and immediately came to Matthew 6:25, where Jesus tells us not to worry about anything, for the heavenly Father knows we need food, clothing, and shelter." The impressions of that moment have never left her, and it was that experience that taught her to appreciate the power of God's Word for daily strength.

At the same time, Janice developed a new love and appreciation for the church.

"The next day was Sunday," she said, "so my husband and I went to church in borrowed clothing and hid up in the balcony. At the end of the service, the pastor talked about our misfortune and took up a special offering for us. The next day as we were shopping to replace underwear and school clothes, he found us in the mall and handed us a check that still brings tears to my eyes when I think about it."

Janice also learned the power of prayer. "Our biggest problem was paying for the trailer, for we had borrowed money for the purchase. Since we were eleven days late on our insurance payment, there was no coverage, and I had visions of making payments for the next thirty years on a trailer that had burned down almost as soon as we had moved into it." She was praying earnestly about this, she told me, one day while driving home from work, and as she entered the house her husband greeted her with news that the mortgage company had called unexpectedly to say they were covering the balance of the loan.

Many years have passed since that cold winter in North Dakota, but Janice still thanks God for the lessons she learned and for the way God provided. That experience taught her to face life as a tough-minded optimist, leaning fully on the promise of Romans 8:28.

We Know

Notice the first two words of this verse: "*We know* that all things work together for good to those who love God. . . ."

The words *we know* are not necessary to the promise, and the verse makes perfect sense without them. If it simply read "All things work together for good to those who love God," we would never have been the wiser, and it still would have been a great truth. In fact, if the verse were worded like that, the primary subject and verb would be the promise itself: (All) Things/Work!

But the Holy Spirit, who doesn't waste words in the Bible, began the sentence, not with an emphasis on what God is going to do, but with an emphasis on what our attitude should be about it. The primary subject is the pronoun *we,* and the primary verb is *know.* Romans 8:28 thus begins with a statement of certitude, underscoring how important it is to God that we claim His promise with total confidence.

We don't hope, hypothesize, or hallucinate. We don't postulate, speculate, or fabricate. We don't toss and turn in anxiety. We simply know. We know God, therefore we know His power, understand something of His providence, and can trust His provision.

It's certain. For sure. Positive. Fail-safe. Inevitable. It's God's guarantee, and it can never be otherwise.

This is an attitude we see throughout Scripture. The word *know* occurs 1,098 times from Genesis to Revelation, and we're instructed to approach life with total trust in the realities of Christ.

- "'I *know* that my Redeemer lives, and that in the end he will stand upon the earth'" (Job 19:25 NIV).
- "I have written these things to you who believe in the name of the son of God, so that you may *know* that you have eternal life" (1 John 5:13).

- "*Know* that the LORD is God" (Ps. 100:3a NIV).
- "'*Know*, then, that not a word the LORD spoke . . . will fail, for the LORD has done what He promised . . . .'" (2 Kings 10:10).
- "*Know* that the LORD has set apart the faithful for Himself" (Ps. 4:3a).
- "'*Know* that Yahweh your God is God, the faithful God who keeps His gracious covenant'" (Deut. 7:9a).
- "'We have come to believe and *know* that You are the Holy One of God!'" (John 6:69).
- "We *know* that when He appears, we will be like Him" (1 John 3:2b).
- "You *know* that He was revealed so that He might take away sins" (1 John 3:5a).
- "You *know* the grace of our Lord Jesus Christ: although He was rich, for your sake He became poor, so that by His poverty you might become rich" (2 Cor. 8:9).
- "'You will *know* the truth, and the truth will set you free'" (John 8:32).
- "'One thing I do *know*: I was blind, and now I can see!'" (John 9:25b).

Tackling Life with Confidence

Faith is the ability to tackle life with confidence, come what may, knowing that the trustworthy promises of God are precisely as real as the transient circumstances around us. Faith is believing that God will do exactly as He has said. Living by faith isn't a matter of sticking our heads in the sand and hoping for the best. It's confronting the realities of life from the perspective of God's immutable, unbreakable, unfailing Word. Those who live by faith don't have a "hope so" optimism. They live in the society of the certain.

Yes, the Bible does use the word *hope*. But in the Bible, hope is not synonymous with *maybe*. Biblical hope refers to sure and certain expectations, which, because they're still in the future, create in us a sense of anticipation.

Pretend you are a Superhero whose claim to fame is the supernatural ability to see one hour into the future. One day you attend a football game. Using your ability, you know for certain at halftime that your team is going to kick a final field goal and win the game in the closing seconds of the fourth quarter. Sitting in the stands, you'd still cheer and jump to your feet, but when the score goes against the players in the third quarter, you wouldn't get discouraged. When the opposing team scores back-to-back touchdowns, you wouldn't despair. The sense of uncertainty would be gone, and you could shrug off setbacks because your special insight tells you that everything will turn out well in the end.

That's not a perfect illustration, but it helps us understand the nature of biblical hope and the possibility of living with confidence even when things seem to be going against us. We don't know exactly what will happen from moment to moment, and we can't call the plays in advance. But we know the final score is 8–28.

Michael Faraday was an English chemist and physicist whose discoveries and theories helped lay the foundation of modern physics. His experiments in electricity and electromagnetism led to landmark discoveries, and his discovery in 1845 that an intense magnetic field can rotate the plane of polarized light is still known as the "Faraday Effect."

In August of 1867, as Faraday lay on his deathbed, journalists were eager to interview the great professor, trying to elicit a final story for their newspapers. One of them asked him as he lay dying, "What are your speculations?"

"Speculations?" replied the doctor indignantly. "Speculations! I have none! I am resting on certainties. *I know* whom I have believed and am persuaded that He is able to keep that which I have committed unto Him against that day."[1]

Pity the poor fellow who goes through life relying on speculations in the great matters of life and death. The American folk philosopher Robert Fulghum, author of *All I Really Need to Know I Learned in Kindergarten,* confessed that by his fifties, he had distilled his credo—his rock-bottom beliefs—into a single word: Maybe.[2]

Christians don't live on mights or maybes.

We *know* our Redeemer lives. We *know* we have eternal life. We *know* the truth. We *know* Him and we are persuaded that nothing can separate us from His love. And therefore we *know* that all things work together for our good.

Perhaps circumstances are overwhelming you like a tsunami of sorrow. Maybe you're facing a medical catastrophe, a financial disaster, a relationship crisis, or unexpected bereavement. Maybe a loved one is in crisis, a child is on drugs, or your husband is battling alcoholism. Maybe you've committed a grave error or made a huge mistake. Perhaps today you lost your job.

These are not good things, and it takes time to process them. We aren't unaffected by their intensity. It takes a while to adjust to new, unwelcome realities, and our emotions are sometimes slow to recover. That was true of the heroes of Scripture, too, and even of the Lord Jesus Christ. More than once in the Gospels we see Him anguished and sorrowing. But in the end, the promise of Romans 8:28 wins out, and faith is the victory.

There's a verse in the Bible that serves as the polar opposite of Romans 8:28, and it was spoken by the patriarch Jacob in

---

1. F. W. Boreham, *A Handful of Stars* (Philadelphia: Judson Press, 1922), 183–84.
2. Robert Fulghum, *Words I Wish I Wrote* (New York: Cliff Street Books, 1997), 3.

Genesis 42. Jacob, an old man and feeble, had suffered a series of blows that would have knocked the life out of anyone. His sons had caused him nothing but trouble, and some of their actions were truly despicable. His dearest and truest son, Joseph, had been killed by a wild animal and eaten—or so Jacob thought. He was facing economic ruin because of a famine, and his sons had gone to Egypt looking for food and, in the process, had created in international incident that had left one of them rotting in an Egyptian prison. Jacob's youngest son, Benjamin, was heading out on a dangerous mission to try to free him, and Jacob was overwhelmed with foreboding and fear.

In verse 36, he gave vent to his feelings: "You have bereaved me: Joseph is no more, Simeon is no more, and you want to take Benjamin. All these things are against me" (NKJV).

Notice that phrase: "All these things are against me."

Now, notice Romans 8:28: "all things work together for good."

The first statement reflects how we feel from our perspective; the second describes how things really are from God's perspective.

And as it turned out, all the things that seemed to be against Jacob really did become things that worked together for good. Joseph wasn't dead after all; he was the prime minister of Egypt. The famine was God's tool to reunite father and son. The brother held hostage became the mechanism for family reconciliation. And the very events that so distressed Jacob were the circumstances that catapulted his family to prosperity and set the stage for all subsequent Old Testament history.

At the outset of every crisis or problem, we have to choose our attitude. Either we'll collapse in despair and say, "All these things are against me." Or we'll decide to view them through the prism of Romans 8:28 and say, "All these things may appear to be against me, but according to God's Word, all these things will work themselves out for my good in God's timing and providence."

Genesis 42:36	Romans 8:28
"Their father Jacob said to them, 'You have bereaved me of my children: Joseph is no more, and Simeon is no more, and you would take Benjamin; <u>all these things are against me</u>'" (NASB).	"And we know that God causes <u>all things to work together for good</u> to those who love God, to those who are called according to His purpose" (NASB).

This explained the attitude of Dr. Bernard Gilpin, a Christian hero of an earlier day who had a reputation for cheerfulness and was often heard quoting this verse to his people. Gilpin, born in 1517, the same year Martin Luther sparked the Protestant Reformation, was a great evangelist in the British Isles, working especially in the remote areas of Great Britain. He was dubbed the "Apostle to the North," but to his parishioners he was the Romans 8:28 man.

One day during his travels, he broke his leg in an accident. Someone mockingly asked if his broken leg would turn out for his good. "Yes," Gilpin replied vigorously, "all things."

And so it did. His broken leg delayed his trip to London where the queen, "Bloody" Mary, had determined to place him on trial because of his preaching. By the time he was able to resume his journey, the news came that Mary had died. Gilpin was saved from almost certain martyrdom, and he lived to serve the Lord with renewed freedom for another twenty-five years.[3]

We should all be Romans 8:28 people. This is a verse that never falters and a promise that cannot fail. For *we know* that all things work together for the good of those who love God: those who are called according to His purpose.

3. G. M. Alexander, *Changes for the Better* (Sheffield, S. Yorks, England: Zoar Publications, n.d.), 11–12.

*God would never permit evil
if He could not bring good out of evil.*
—Augustine

CHAPTER 5

All Things

We know that all things work together
for the good of those who love God:
those who are called according to His purpose.

I recently attended a retirement dinner honoring a friend of mine who had built a great company from the ground up. His colleagues and coworkers rose to pay tribute to him, but the speaker who impressed me most was his successor in the company. The two men had worked together for several years. "We've had good times and bad times," said the incoming CEO, "and occasionally it was my duty to bring negative financial reports to our meetings. I'd approach Sam's office with apprehension because I didn't like being the bearer of bad news. But Sam would study the reports, look up, and say, 'Let me ask you, my friend, is Romans 8:28 still in the Bible?'"

"Yes, to the best of my knowledge it is, Sam."

"Then this will turn around; it will all work out for good. Don't be discouraged."

That was his working philosophy, and it's no wonder he was respected around the world for his leadership, vision, and optimism.

All things include bad financial reports, personal mistakes, misunderstandings, and even tragedies. The great Bible teacher Dr. Martyn Lloyd-Jones drove this home in his lectures from Romans 8:

> God can make all, and does make all, work ultimately for our good. This is surely a staggering statement; but it is the statement that is made by the Apostle. It is only in the case of Christians that we can demonstrate exactly how this happens, how all things are made to work together for our good. Trials and tribulations and failures and sin are not good in and of themselves, and it is folly to pretend that they are. They are bad. How then can we justify the statement that all of them "work together for good"? The answer is that they are so used by God, and so over-ruled by God and employed by God that they turn out for our good.[1]

My office is lined with bookcases, and the books I enjoy the most are those filled with biographies and autobiographies. I've collected many volumes by and about great Christians from every era of church history. Every one of these biographies, without exception, is a representation of this truth. Every biography is filled with moments of anguish, uncertainty, tragedy, and disappointment—and with subsequent events that remarkably caused it all, in the end, to turn out so well that it was worth recording in book form. Each of these accounts is an unfailing demonstration of Romans 8:28, as if that verse were written on the front page of every book.

Romans 8:28 is the banner suspended over every Christian's life. It's printed on our birth certificates when we're born and

---

1. David Martyn Lloyd-Jones, *Romans: The Final Perseverance of the Saints: Expositions of Chapters 8:17–39* (Grand Rapids, MI: Zondervan, 1975), 164.

inscribed on our tombstones when we die. For God's people who love Him and are called according to His purpose, it's the flag that flies over the castle of our lives.

Several years ago, I picked up Catherine Marshall's memoirs *To Live Again* and couldn't put it down. The sudden death of her husband, Peter Marshall, chaplain of the U. S. Senate, left Catherine with black-banded grief, mounting problems, financial pressures, and a young fatherless son. In her despair she groped for a way of coping with her nightmare.

> I remembered a technique that Peter had often used. It was the method of finding a specific promise in the Bible that applied to one's need and then claiming it as a definite transaction between an individual and his Lord. A favorite quotation had often been on Peter's lips at such a time of claiming. He had written it on the flyleaf of his Bible. It was a statement of David Livingstone, the Scottish missionary and explorer of Africa . . . "It is the word of a Gentleman of the most sacred and strictest honor, and there is an end on't."
>
> In precisely that spirit I claimed for myself and the son whom Peter and I had brought into the world the promise: "And we know that all things [the things we understand and those we do not; the joyous things and the tragic] work together for good to them that love God, to them that are the called according to His purpose."[2]

As Catherine recounted her recovery from despair and grief, this verse became a turning point in her life, and she went on to become one of the best—and one of the best-selling—authors of

2. Catherine Marshall, *To Live Again* (New York: McGraw-Hill, 1957), 36–37.

the twentieth century. Notice how she interpreted the word *all:* "the things we understand and those we do not; the joyous things and the tragic."

The Biggest Little Word

Romans 8:28 is an all-inclusive promise. Nothing is excluded from the invitation. No problem is too small for His notice; none is too large for His power. The tremendous events of life and the tragic ones. Each and every problem is His concern. He can handle them, and we're to give them all to Him in total trust, for His is the word of a perfect gentleman.

All is the biggest word in this verse. Not some things, a few things, a lot of things, select things, good things, bad things, sad things, or funny things—but all things. There is no asterisk on the word "all." There are no exceptions or exemptions. It's neither hyperbole nor exaggeration. If it were not all-encompassing, it wouldn't be worth the paper it's printed on. All means all.

As it turns out, all is one of God's favorite words.

One evening about a year ago when I was troubled about a particular matter, I sat down at the dining room table and read through the little book of 1 Peter near the back of the Bible, thinking the old fisherman might have an encouraging word for me. When I got to the last chapter, I came across verse 7: "Casting all your care upon Him, because He cares about you." It was a verse I knew well, indeed had memorized, but now I saw something I'd never seen before. It said: "Casting *all* your care upon Him."

Then a thought came to me. I wondered if there were other *all*s in the Bible I'd missed. Continuing my reading, I noticed three verses later that God is "the God of all grace." Four verses later: "Peace to all of you." Further on, in 2 Peter 1:3, I read, "His divine power has given to us all things that pertain to life and godliness, through the knowledge of Him who called us" (NKJV).

Looking up the word in a concordance, I was amazed to find 5,675 uses of *all* in the Bible. I realized that this word shows up in a remarkable number of verses, and it modifies many of the greatest truths, commands, and promises of the Bible.[3]

Believe it or not, I looked up all the *all*s of Scripture, finding it to be one of my most encouraging Bible studies ever. *All* is such a common little word that we're apt to overlook its appearance. For example, notice these other sightings in Romans 8:

- "He who did not spare His own Son, but delivered Him up for us *all,* how shall He not with Him also freely give us *all* things?" (v. 32 NKJV).
- "No, in *all* these things we are more than victorious through Him who loved us" (v. 37).
- "For I am persuaded that neither death nor life, nor angels nor principalities nor powers, nor things present nor things to come, nor height nor depth, nor any other created thing, shall be able to separate us from the love of God which is in Christ Jesus our Lord" (vv. 38–39 NKJV).

Since *all* things work together for good and since God graciously gives *all* of us *all* things, we are more than conquerors in *all* circumstances, and nothing in *all* creation can separate us from His love.

The frequency of this word in Scripture speaks to the all-sufficiency of our almighty Savior. It speaks of the omni qualities of God and of the complete devotion we should afford Him. He is our All-in-All, our Almighty, our all-embracing, all-encompassing, all-sufficient Savior.

---

3. This study is the basis for my book *God's All-Sufficient Grace,* to be released in 2008 by B & H Publishing Group.

Even Our Faults and Failures

Remarkably, the "all things" in this verse includes our sins and failures, when placed under the blood of Christ. Sometimes we exclude those, saying, "I know God can take the things that happen to me and work them out for good, but I've caused this problem myself. I really messed up. I've ruined my home. I've ruined my marriage. I've failed with my children. I've yielded to a dark and terrible temptation. I lost my temper and lost my job. I ran up that debt. This mess is mine alone, and God could not possibly want to bring good out of such a foul and sordid mess as mine."

But He does, if and when we bring our sordid messes to Him in humble repentance and place them under the redeeming blood of Jesus. Looking back at my own experience, I realize that some of my old sins—now confessed, pardoned, forgiven, and cleansed—have equipped me to effectively counsel others currently battling the same temptation.

It's because of David's sin with Bathsheba—his adultery, murder, and cover-up—that we have precious Psalm 51. Remarkably, it's also from the subsequent marriage of these two adulterers that God brought forth the messianic line through Solomon.

It's because of Peter's sin in cursing and denying Christ on the eve of our Lord's crucifixion that we can relate so powerfully to him. And it was the recollection of his failure that led to the renewed threefold commitment he made to the risen Christ by the seashore in John 21. In the book of Acts, his intrepidity in preaching was, to some extent, because of his determination to never again falter in the face of persecution. It's similar to when the doctor tells you that your broken bone, once set and healed, will be stronger than it was before the fracture.

Perhaps the most amazing demonstration of this involves the story of the nation of Judah in the Old Testament. God's chosen people—heirs of the covenant—so sinned against Him they were driven from the land, their nation was disassembled, and the survivors were scattered among the nations. Yet in the unfolding of God's providence, the tiny nation of Israel was reborn long enough for the Messiah to be born. Even then, however, the vast majority of Jews were of the Diaspora—dispersed among the nations. There they formed synagogues. When the gospel began to expand beyond Jerusalem and Judea, the early missionaries like Peter and Paul found a foothold for their ministry in these synagogues. Going to a town or city, they would first go to the synagogue. Throughout the Roman Empire, the presence of the Jews in every province provided monotheistic beachheads for the gospel, without which it could not have spread.

God hates evil, but His purposes and decrees are not stymied by it. Whether in human history or in the individual lives of His children, His "deeper magic," to use C. S. Lewis's phrase, turns bad things inside out and uses them for good.

It was Augustine's prodigal years that made him such a passionate thinker. It was Bunyan's filthy mouth that, after his conversion, became a fount of blessing. His written words are immortalized in *Pilgrim's Progress*. It was the sordid life of John Newton that prompted him, after his conversion, to give the world "Amazing Grace."

And God's grace still amazes us, for even our hang-ups, sins, and moral failures are part of the "all things" of Romans 8:28 when nailed to the cross of Jesus Christ.

Were It Not for Grace

One of the organizations I most admire is Wycliffe Bible Translators, and in Wycliffe's history are two airplane crashes that bear out the truth of Romans 8:28. In 1946, there was a young family of three souls who needed to be transported by plane from their missionary station in Peru to Mexico City. Their names were Cameron Townsend, his wife, Helen, and their six-week-old daughter, Grace. Cameron was the founder of Wycliffe Bible Translators, and they were going to Mexico City to visit recruits at one of the training centers.

A young, inexperienced pilot came to pick them up in a Piper Super Cruiser, and the young family squeezed into the cabin. They went bouncing down the runway and took off, but the pilot banked the plane too soon, and the tail of the plane struck the top of a tree, sending the aircraft crashing into a ravine. The pilot survived but was unconscious for several days. Cameron survived with injuries. Helen survived, but her leg was nearly severed. Thankfully, the baby survived unhurt.

As Cameron waited for the stretcher, a powerful thought came into his mind. There has got to be a reliable and safe missionary aviation service for Bible translators going into the jungle. During his recuperation, his plans took shape, and later an organization was born known as the Jungle Aviation and Radio Service, or JAARS. Today JAARS is one of the greatest and most unusual transport services in the world, ferrying missionaries, translators, and humanitarian workers to the most remote spots on earth.

Had there been no mistake, there would have been no crash; and had there been no crash, there might never have been a jungle aviation program. But the story doesn't end there.

The years passed, and JAARS had a remarkable safety record. Its pilots logged millions of miles in all kinds of weather, ferrying passengers to unmapped spots in the jungles of South America, Asia, and other places. They boasted twenty-five years without a fatality.

Then in 1972, tragedy stuck. A missionary pilot named Doug Hunt returned from a much-needed vacation and resumed his work by taking the controls of an Aztec aircraft, heading toward the Wycliffe center in Ukarumpa, Papua New Guinea. The plane carried seven people, including a noted and brilliant missionary linguist. Doug took off, and the plane reached an altitude of 6,500 feet. Suddenly, Doug saw a brilliant flash out his right window and realized the engine was on fire. He brought all his skills to bear, sending a mayday signal and trying to find a place to land the plane; but he lost control, and the Aztec began spiraling downward. It lost six thousand feet in two minutes, and Doug tried to level off about one hundred feet above the ground. There was another brilliant flash of light, and the plane began breaking apart. The next instant, the seven people on board were with the Lord.

Back at the Ukarumpa station, a man named Ken Wiggers received the tragic news by radio transmission while the Wycliffe family was in the middle of a church service. As he approached the little building, he heard the sounds of joyful singing, and he dreaded his task. Pushing the door open, he interrupted the service and broke the news that their friends and family members had died in the plane crash.

As Ken finished, someone else took over the service and began comforting the family and friends of those who had perished, and Ken, who had immediate tasks to attend to, left the building. As he did so, someone burst out of the shadows and grabbed him by the shirt, holding on to him and weeping uncontrollably. It was one of the mechanics. The man said, "I was sitting there in that meeting, wracking my brain trying to remember. Now I know. It was my fault. The whole thing is my fault."

This mechanic went on to explain that the day before he had worked on the engine, and as he was finishing hooking up the fuel line, another worker asked for his help. He had tightened the nut on the fuel line with his fingers and had intended to give the nut one extra twist with the wrench but had forgotten to go back and do it. The lack of that final twist of the wrench meant that a fine spray of gasoline could have escaped, struck the hot engine, and ignited.

A subsequent investigation revealed that was exactly what had happened.

This mechanic was nearly suicidal in his anguish over his tragic mistake. When he saw the seven caskets lined up in the little tropical church a few days later, it nearly drove him insane. He later said, "(It) hit me in the stomach. I wanted nothing but to get out of there. . . . How could I face my friends? How could I face myself? I was overwhelmed with guilt. I was a failure."

A few days later he forced himself to sit down with the widow of the pilot, and through sobs and tears he confessed his error. He looked at his right hand and told her, "That hand there took Doug's life." Mrs. Hunt took his hand and held it in her own, and she extended her full love, comfort, and forgiveness. That was the significant first step in the healing process.

Some time later, Jamie Buckingham wrote a history of JAARS titled *Into the Glory,* and he devoted a chapter to this story. Thousands of people were inspired and moved by the story, and some gave their lives to missionary service.

This is what the mechanic later wrote: "Time went on and heart-healing continued. But it was a long time before I could talk about the accident. In fact, not until after I learned how God was blessing lives as a result of the book about JAARS—*Into the Glory* by Jamie Buckingham—did I realize my story could be a blessing to others. Readers seemed to find a special encouragement in the chapter about the Aztec crash and a young mechanic who thought he was a failure, but God kept him going."

Then he said this: "Except for God's grace I'd be somewhere cowering in a corner in guilt-ridden despair—the eighth fatality of the Aztec crash."[4]

"Except for God's grace . . ."

It reminds me of the song by Larnelle Harris that says:

> Were it not for grace
> I can tell you where I'd be . . .
> Forever running but losing this race
> Were it not for grace

I believe that when Jesus Christ died on the cross of Calvary, His blood was an acid strong enough to dispense with all our sin and guilt, and His grace was a force strong enough to turn our sorrows into songs. His redemption covers both our sins and our mistakes—and everything in between. For by His stripes we are healed.

If you've made mistakes in your life, don't wallow in them anymore. Write Romans 8:28 over that page in your story. Give your foul-ups to God. Claim His promise that *all things* work together for good to those who love Him and are called according to His purpose. Claim the promise of Ephesians 1:11 that God works all things together according to the counsel of His will. Give all to Him and trust His grace.

He alone knows how to turn poison into porridge, mistakes into masterpieces, snafus into songs, and errors into alleluias.

---

4. Jamie Buckingham, *Into the Glory* (Plainfield, NJ: Logos International, 1974), chap. 18. Ruth A. Tucker, *From Jerusalem to Irian Jaya* (Grand Rapids, MI: Academie Books, 1983), 403–4. Also see www.jaars.org and www.bible.org/illus.asp?topic_id=576.

We believe in the providence of God,
but we do not believe half enough in it. . . .
All the mysterious arrangements
of providence work for our good.
—Charles Spurgeon

CHAPTER 6

Work Together

We know that all things work together
for the good of those who love God:
those who are called according to His purpose.

As a college student, Kevin Harper served as my intern, and I found him to be bright, friendly, and hard-working. When he moved to Oklahoma, I felt I'd lost a friend, but he's kept in touch with me ever since, calling me frequently and letting me know what's going on in his life. Some of those calls have made me wince, like the time his car flipped over three times on the freeway, sending him to the hospital, and the time he fell off a fifty-foot cliff during a rappelling trip. His harness broke and he plunged to the ground like a rock. That particular crisis took considerable recovery time, but Kevin's attitude is unsinkable, and he seasons his life with the herbs of joy and contentment.

Several years ago, however, Kevin's optimism was put to the test when he and his wife, Jennifer, suffered a tragic miscarriage. Their doctor subsequently told them to abandon their hopes of having children, but soon another child was on the way, and they were overjoyed.

Some time later, Kevin called to tell me that little Jaxson had been born, but things hadn't gone well in the delivery room. The tiny fellow had "crashed" three times right out of the womb, and a medical team had literally run through the halls, carrying the baby and virtually dragging Kevin to a neonatal intensive care unit. Kevin described the awful fear that had gripped him at that moment, and about the panic Jennifer had felt, lying helplessly in the delivery room as her baby was whisked away.

Recently, Kevin called with an update. "These have been the best and the worst thirteen days of our lives," he said. "We love this little boy so very much, but last night we told him, 'If it's better for you to go be with Jesus, then go on; that's what you should do.'"

Then he said, his voice breaking, "Jaxson's dying, Rob. He's going on to be with Jesus, and I'm going to preach at his memorial service, and I believe that God has a purpose in this and that great good will come from it."

As I hung up the phone, a stream of sadness cut a channel through my heart. I didn't feel like working anymore; I felt tired and sad. Reaching to the shelf above my desk, I pulled down John Oxenham's little volume of poems *Bees in Amber* and read once again his verse titled "God's Handwriting."

> He writes in characters too grand
> For our short sight to understand;
> We catch but broken strokes, and try
> To fathom all the mystery
> Of withered hopes, of death, of life,
> The endless war, the useless strife,—
> But there, with larger, clearer sight,
> We shall see this—His way was right.[1]

---

1. John Oxenham, *Bees in Amber* (American Tract Society, 1913), 37.

We don't always feel that God's way is right, but His faithfulness doesn't depend on our vacillating emotions, rather on His unchanging Word. It's not a matter of how we feel but of what God says. Romans 8:28, like all of God's promises, must be claimed and appropriated *by faith,* for we can't always make sense of it *by sight.* As time goes by, of course, we can look back and discern some of God's "handwriting" and see some of the wonderful purposes and patterns of His providence. As Søren Kierkegaard famously said, "Life must be lived forward; it can only be understood backwards."

At the moment of crying or crisis, however, we must focus on only the promise, even if we can't see God's pattern, understand His purpose, or feel His peace.

"When you can't trace His hand," said Charles Spurgeon, "you can trust His heart."

That knowledge may or may not salvage our emotions at the moment of crisis, but it does represent a fundamental shift in the substructures of our attitudes, and it sets the stage for eventual healing and ultimate joy.

Romans 8:28 was originally written in the Greek language, and the word used here is *synergeō,* from which we get our modern word *synergy.* It means "to work together with." There is an irresistible law of divine synergy operational in the God-lover's life, working together all things to produce effects greater than and often completely different from the sum of the various elements. This synergy works under the authority of God's undeniable providence.

Dr. Handley Moule was a brilliant British Bible teacher and author who died in 1920. On one occasion, he was called to the scene of a terrible accident at a British coal mine. Many friends and relatives of the victims of the cave-in gathered, and it was Dr. Moule's responsibility to address them.

"It is very difficult," he said, "for us to understand why God should let an awful disaster happen, but we know Him and trust Him, and all will be right. I have at home an old bookmarker given me by my mother. It is worked in silk, and when I examine the wrong side of it, I see nothing but a tangle of threads. It looks like a big mistake. One would think that someone had done it who did not know what she was doing. But when I turn it over and look at the right side, I see there, beautifully embroidered, the letters, 'God is love!' We are looking at all this today from the wrong side. Some day we shall see it from another standpoint and we shall understand."[2]

Sometimes in the face of tragedy and disappointment, we can only hide ourselves in the promises of God until the storm passes by. We have to reassure our heart with the facts of God when we can't calculate the sums of life. We have to tell ourselves the truth, regardless of appearances to the contrary: Not some things, but *all* things work together.

I once heard it likened to a man who takes the back off his wristwatch. There are gears and flywheels going in all directions, and it seems counterintuitive to think that as one gear goes one way and the other goes in the opposite direction, the hands on the dial move forward at exactly the right speed. Yet that's how it works.

And that's how it's worked in my own life. My wife and I were married on August 28, 1976. Twenty-five years later, we had planned to spend our silver wedding anniversary on a cruise. When those plans fell apart, we looked around Nashville to see what we could enjoy doing on that day. The only special event in town was at the Opryland Hotel—the exhibition of items salvaged from the *Titanic*.

---

2. Walter B. Knight, *Knight's Master Book of New Illustrations* (Grand Rapids, MI: Eerdmans, 1973), 584–85.

Well, that wasn't quite what we had in mind, but we decided to put a good face to it and go. Then, as the morning dawned, we were hit by bad news. It was one of those moments when you're powerless. There was nothing we could do, for it was a situation beyond our control. But it still affected our moods, mine especially. I was so downcast in my spirits that I dreaded the whole day and wondered how I could ever enjoy celebrating our anniversary or anything else.

That's when my friend Brian Swartz happened to call, wishing us a happy anniversary. I told him what had happened, and I'll never forget his reply.

"Rob, think about it," he said. "This is your anniversary: August 28th. How do you abbreviate that on your letterhead? This is 8/28/01—the eighth month and the twenty-eighth day—8/28, as in Romans 8:28. All the things you're worried about this morning are going to work together for good. Now, take your wife out for the day, brighten your attitude, trust the Lord's promise, and let me do the praying today."

In all honesty, I didn't manage many celebratory feelings that day, but I did get my emotions off the floor. Katrina and I put our troubles on hold, and we went to the *Titanic* exhibition and thought of those people who, on April 14, 1912, had problems far greater than ours. We marveled at the opulence of the *Titanic,* shuddered at the terror of its fate, and even bought a small lump of coal salvaged from its rusting hull.

Six years have passed, and the crisis of that day is long past. Everything has worked out reasonably well, and I've often shared the story of Brian's phone call with others. The memory of his message is precious to me, for it reminded me that every day is 8/28, and this promise works 24/7.

It isn't merely a life preserver; it actually puts cork into our very souls. We become unsinkable people because of our God whose promises are unfailing, even in rough seas. The promise of Romans 8:28 enables us to keep our heads above the water even when our ship seems to be going down.

CHAPTER 7

For Good

**We know that all things work together
for the good** of those who love God:
those who are called according to His purpose.

In my church in Nashville there's a wonderful man named Ron Meyers, a retired missionary who invested his life and career for Christ in Congo. When Ron heard I was studying Romans 8:28, he wanted to tell me a story from his young days. His brother Allen and a friend came in from the field for a meal in the rural Nebraska farmhouse. Their dad joined them, and the men tuned the radio to the evening newscast. The Korean War was raging, and reports weren't good. Replacements were needed for the troops. Allen and his friend seemed particularly attentive and soon afterward enlisted in the Marine Corps and headed off to war.

After a punishing winter on the DMZ, Allen received orders to return to the United States, but on the way home from the battlefront, he stepped on a land mine and was killed instantly. It was a terrible blow to the whole family, but especially to his dad who had expected to transfer the family farm into Allen's capable hands.

Allen's death, however, began to have a great effect on his dad's spiritual life. Before this time, Ron told me, his father had shown little interest in spiritual matters and was at best a largely silent Christian.

"But a few years later," Ron said, "I recall milking cows along-side my dad in the barn, and we had a wonderful talk about spiritual things. By this time, my dad was a committed follower of Christ. 'You know, Ron,' he said, 'before Allen was killed I didn't think about these things.'"

Ron's father went on to become a door-to-door Bible sales agent, and he joined the Gideons to help distribute New Testaments in public schools. He became a strong supporter of missionaries—including Ron and his sister who both served the Lord overseas. Farming was no longer the ultimate reason for the family's existence, for now they were using a variety of means to spread the gospel throughout the world. They were changing eternity.

"Looking back to the loss of his beloved son," Ron said, "it was that event that somehow led my father to choose Romans 8:28 as his favorite verse. He took it as a personal promise from God. It gave him a new attitude in life, and it became his favorite verse in all the Bible. It literally kept him going."

The truth of Romans 8:28 keeps us going because it's backed by the redeeming blood of Christ and is an important component of God's redemptive power. When Adam and Eve sinned, a curse fell over the human race and all things worked for bad. In fact, without Jesus Christ, everything still works together for bad. That's the seldom-mentioned flip side of Romans 8:28. If you were to hold the verse up to a mirror to read its opposite reflection, it would say: "We know that all things work to the detriment of those who don't know the Lord and who aren't called according to His purpose."

Such people often appear to have great success. They strike

it rich, arrive at pinnacles of power, amass great fortunes, and accomplish impressive results. But ultimately and inevitably, it all conspires for their own detriment and destruction if Christ Jesus isn't their Lord and Savior. As the Puritan Thomas Watson put it: "To them that are godly, evil things work for good; to them that are evil, good things work for hurt."[1]

Jesus died on the cross to give us Romans 8:28. The Lord Himself became a human, entering the world through the virgin's womb. The God of glory became the Man of Sorrows, bearing the evils of the world and shedding His blood to provide redemption. "For you know," wrote Peter, "that it was not with perishable things such as silver or gold that you were redeemed from the empty way of life handed down to you from your forefathers, but with the precious blood of Christ, a lamb without blemish or defect" (1 Pet. 1:18–19 NIV).

The word *redeem* involves the idea of a ransom, of buying back. Christians are redeemed from their debt of sin by the perfect atonement accomplished by our Lord Jesus as recorded in the Gospels and explained in Romans. We are purchased by His blood, and our souls are redeemed. But Christ's redemption goes beyond the spiritual; it extends to all our life situations. His blood, like a rampaging flood, carries all our circumstances into the channels of God's redemptive grace. So not only do our sins fall under the pardon of His blood, our cares are swallowed up in His providence.

Dr. R. C. Sproul wrote, "While the popular adage declares that 'the devil is in the details,' it is more accurate to avow that God is in the details. The doctrine of providence declares that God's providential rule extends to all things great and small, from the huge to the minute, the infinite to the infinitesimal."

---

1. Thomas Watson, *A Divine Cordial* (1663; repr., Lafayette, IN: Sovereign Grace, 2001), 43.

Someone has called providence "the hidden hand of God." It is God's invisible hand behind the curtains of life, aligning the circumstances, bringing victory from the jaws of defeat, turning tables on the Devil's schemes, and ensuring that all things work together for good for His children. He undergirds the good and overrules the bad. That's providence.

Historical Providence

There are two sides to this doctrine of providence. Historical providence is God's providential control of human history. This is the theme of one whole book in the Bible—the Old Testament account of Esther. When you read Esther, you'll not find the word God anywhere, nor is there any reference to Him. The story is about the survival of the Jewish people during the days of the Persian Empire when they faced annihilation. Somehow the right people—Mordecai and Esther—found themselves in royal circles at exactly the right times, and through a risky game of political brinkmanship, they managed to save the Jews.

One commentary puts it this way: "The book of Esther is an exciting story that is a living illustration of the unseen hand of God's providence. Although the name of God is not mentioned in the entire narrative, His overruling sovereignty is seen in every event."[2]

This is also the core concept running like a ribbon through the books of Daniel and Revelation. Even when God is nowhere in sight, even when He is acknowledged by neither small nor great, even when history appears to be lurching from one disaster to the next, even when the wrong side prevails, even *then* God is in control, funneling people and events into the channel of His pre-appointed and foreordained ends. "Despots may plan and armies

---

2. *The KJV Bible Commentary* (Nashville: Thomas Nelson, 1997, c1994), S. 909.

may march, and the congresses of the nations may seem to think they are adjusting all the affairs of the world, but the mighty men of the earth are only the dust of the chariot wheels of God's providence," declared Brooklyn pastor T. DeWitt Talmage.[3]

In my study of the Bible, there are two phrases that I love. In 1 Kings 12, we have the story of King Rehoboam who made a strategic blunder shortly after assuming the throne. The result was the division of the nation of Israel, an event that has shaped Jewish history ever since. But one little phrase in 1 Kings 12:15 lets us know that even the tragic blunders of shortsighted leaders can accomplish God's plan: *"The turn of events came from the Lord."*

The other phrase is even shorter. In Daniel 4:26, the entire doctrine of providence and the whole of the book of Daniel is summarized in two words: *"Heaven rules."*

In more recent times, one narrow body of water demonstrated this—the English Channel. In the sixteenth century, Spain's King Philip II, an arch-Catholic, wanted to topple Protestantism in England and abort the reign of the Protestant Queen Elizabeth I. He readied his navy, the largest and strongest on earth, for invasion. On May 30, 1588, he fell to his knees before his "invincible" armada, prayed for victory, and watched it disappear over the horizon. But providence sided with the English. The Spanish armada was quickly hurled in every direction by a violent storm. The beleaguered fleet regrouped, pressed on, and was spotted by the British on July 19. Winds turned against the armada, slowing its progress.

When the battle was joined on July 21, weather again aided the English. Heavy winds favored their smaller, more manageable ships. The English outmaneuvered the Spanish, and at precisely the right moments the weather shifted, always in England's favor.

---

3. John Rusk, *The Authentic Life of T. DeWitt Talmage*, © 1902, L. G. Stahl (E. E. Knowles & Co. 1902), 371.

By July 31, the Duke of Parma had informed Philip of likely defeat: "God knows how grieved I am at this news at a time when I hoped to send Your Majesty congratulations. I will only say that this must come from the hand of the Lord, who knows well what He does."

Now fast-forward three centuries.

In 1940, Europe was in the throes of crisis. Poland, Denmark, Norway, Holland, Belgium, and France had all fallen to the Nazi blitzkrieg, forcing the British Expeditionary Force to the sea and trapping it for apparent, inevitable annihilation.

England's King George VI called for a national day of prayer as Churchill's risky evacuation scheme began on May 26. It lasted ten days, during which time the weather behaved oddly. When the dikes were opened to hinder the German advance, the wind blew in from the sea, aiding this strategic move. But had it continued to blow in from the sea, it would have wrecked many of the tiny boats and small vessels transporting soldiers. Instead, the wind blew *as* needed, *where* needed, and *when* needed to facilitate the retreat. And when not needed, it didn't blow. Thousands of troops escaped in an improvised flotilla of tiny vessels only because, through the entire evacuation, the waters of the English Channel were as still as a pond, despite the fact that at the end of May the channel is normally rough and stormy. As an added advantage, the fog rolled in at crucial moments, covering the rescue of the troops.

Churchill described the evacuation as a "miracle of deliverance," and on the following Sunday, the dean of St. Paul's referred to the "Miracle of Dunkirk," a title by which this event is still commonly known. In the days after the evacuation, letters filled the newspapers, reminding the nation that the archbishop of Canterbury had called for a day of national prayer during that time.

The Miracle of Dunkirk saved England's army and, in hindsight, perhaps saved all of England and ultimately the rest of Europe.

History often seems a tangle of events to us, happening helter-skelter, sometimes without rhyme or reason. But the book of Daniel says, "The Most High is ruler over the kingdom of men" (4:25b), and all of history is hurtling toward the preplanned events described in the book of Revelation, guided by an invisible but omnipotent hand.

Personal Providence

The other kind of providence is God's personal providence over the lives of His children. He does for us on a personal and intimate level what He does on a global scale for world history. Some people have called this the unseen hand of God on our lives.

Missionary Frank Laubach (1884–1970) once wrote in his journal: "March 1, 1930: This sense of being led by an unseen hand which takes mine while another hand reaches ahead and prepares the way, grows on me daily."

Charles Spurgeon wrote in his devotional classic *Morning and Evening,* "Let us give to God our hearts, all blazing with love, and seek His grace, that the fire will never be quenched. . . . Many foes will attempt to extinguish it, but if the unseen hand . . . pours the sacred oil, it will blaze higher and higher."[4]

The North Carolina evangelist Vance Havner, who ranked as one of my favorite preachers when I was starting out and with whom I once spent a pleasant afternoon, said this: "I thank God for the Unseen Hand, sometimes urging me onward, sometimes holding me back; sometimes with a caress of approval, sometimes

---

4. Charles H. Spurgeon, *Morning and Evening,* entry for July 15, morning.

with a stroke of reproof; sometimes correcting, sometimes comforting. My times are in His hand. . . . The Unseen Hand may be obscured at times by the fogs of circumstance but just because we can't see the sun on a cloudy day doesn't mean that it isn't there."[5]

When I was working on my book of hymn stories, *Then Sings My Soul,* I became a fan of Fanny Crosby's, who wrote thousands of our favorite songs. She was blinded when she was six weeks old through the malpractice of a doctor. Her mother anguished for years about this, and understandably so. But she also consoled Fanny as the child grew up, telling her that sometimes the Lord permits one of His children to go without the sense of sight or hearing in order for the child to develop his other senses more fully and so fulfill God's purpose in life. So Fanny developed a phenomenal memory, learning much of the Bible by heart. Out of this treasury came a torrent of hymns and gospel songs unequalled in Christian history.

Writing about this in 1903, Fanny said:

> The poor doctor who had spoiled my eyes soon disappeared from the neighborhood and we never heard any more about him. He is probably dead, before this time; but if I could ever meet him, I would tell him that unwittingly he did me the greatest favor in the world.
>
> I have heard that this physician never ceased expressing his regret at the occurrence; and that it was one of the sorrows of his life. But if I could meet him now, I would say, "Thank you, thank you"—over and over again—for making me blind, if it was through your agency that it came about!

5. Vance Havner, *Fourscore* (Old Tappan, NJ: Revell, 1982), 23.

Why would I not have that doctor's mistake—if a mistake it was—remedied? Well, there are many reasons: and I will tell you some of them.

One is that I know, although it may have been a blunder on the physician's part, it was no mistake of God's. I verily believe it was His intention that I should live my days in physical darkness, so as to be better prepared to sing His praises and incite others so to do. I could not have written thousands of hymns—many of which, if you will pardon me for repeating it, are sung all over the world—if I had been hindered by the distractions of seeing all the interesting and beautiful objects that would have been presented to my notice.[6]

It's no wonder that it was Fanny Crosby who wrote the wonderful words of one of my favorite hymns:

> All the way my Savior leads me;
> What have I to ask beside?
> Can I doubt His tender mercy,
> Who through life has been my guide?
> Heavenly peace, divinest comfort,
> Here by faith in Him to dwell!
> For I know whate'er befall me,
> Jesus doeth all things well.

I love that hymn because when I was a junior in college, the senior class, during graduation ceremonies, turned around to face the audience and sang all three verses, and I've never forgotten the effect it had on me. If you love God and are called according to His

---

6. John Loveland, *Blessed Assurance: The Life and Hymns of Fanny J. Crosby* (Nashville: Broadman Press, 1978), 14–15, 21–22.

purpose, Jesus leads you all the way. He's leading you today, work-ing behind you, below you, before you, above you, and within you to accomplish His good will. And we can know, whate'er befall us, that Jesus doeth all things well.

Romans 8:28 is a flower of grace growing on the slopes of Calvary. As Puritan Thomas Watson put it long ago: "To know that nothing hurts the godly is a matter of comfort; but to be assured that ALL things which fall out shall co-operate for their good, that their crosses shall be turned into blessings . . . this may fill their hearts with joy till they run over."[7]

Through the Love of God Our Savior

Through the love of God our Savior,
All will be well;
Free and changeless is His favor;
All, all is well.
Precious is the blood that healed us;
Perfect is the grace that sealed us;
Strong the hand stretched out to shield us;
All must be well.

Though we pass through tribulation,
All will be well;
Ours is such a full salvation;
All, all is well.
Happy still in God confiding,
Fruitful, if in Christ abiding,
Holy through the Spirit's guiding,
All must be well.

---

7. Thomas Watson, *A Divine Cordial* (1663; repr., Lafayette, IN: Sovereign Grace, 2001), 6.

For Good

We expect a bright tomorrow;
All will be well;
Faith can sing through days of sorrow,
All, all is well.
On our Father's love relying,
Jesus every need supplying,
Or in living, or in dying,
All must be well.

—Mary B. Peters (1847)

CHAPTER 8

For Those Who Love God

**We know that all things work together
for the good of those who love God:**
those who are called according to His purpose.

N ow we come to the fine print.

Romans 8:28 isn't a platitude to be slapped on our backsides like a bumper sticker. It's not for universal distribution without conditions, and it's not for wholesale dissemination. It is precisely and only for those who meet the requirement of loving God.

Loving God is the ultimate purpose of the soul. We're made to love, and a life without love is a worthless life. And loving God is the highest duty and the greatest joy of our lives, either in time or eternity. Recently I was deeply impressed as I studied 2 Corinthians 5, the passage in which the apostle Paul talked about dying. He said that to be present in the body is to be absent from the Lord, and to be absent from the body is to be present with the Lord (vv. 6–8). "Therefore," he wrote, "whether we are at home or away, we make it our aim to be pleasing to Him" (v. 9).

What a remarkable passage! When Paul spoke of being at home or away from home, he was talking about being on earth (at home in the body) or in heaven (away from the body). Dead or alive—either way, it doesn't matter in terms of our interest or affections. Whether here or there, whether now or then, we're to love Jesus and want to please Him.

I had wonderful parents, and I always wanted to please them, which is one of the reasons I didn't get into too much trouble as a teenager. Occasionally I had

> ## 2 Cor. 5:6–9
> Therefore, though we are always confident and know that while we are at home in the body we are away from the Lord—for we walk by faith, not by sight—yet we are confident and satisfied to be out of the body and at home with the Lord. Therefore, whether we are at home or away, we make it our aim to be pleasing to Him.

a coach or teacher whose excellence and attentiveness made me want to please him or her. I worked harder in those classes. In my own family, with my wife, daughters, and grandchildren, I want to please them because I love them so much.

We respond to love with love.

Our primary goal each day, then, is to please the One who loves us most. That's my primary purpose in life, to do each day what pleases Him. One day I'm going to have a heart attack, succumb to cancer, die in a car wreck or plane crash, or pass away from old age. But according to 2 Corinthians 5, my life's goal will be unaffected and uninterrupted. It'll be the same in heaven as it is on earth. The driving force of my life won't skip a beat. I'll carry on as before. Whether at home in the body or away from the body, my aim is to please Christ. The other side of death is simply an unbroken continuation of my pursuit, only in a better environment and unfettered by sin. Whether at home or away, our purpose is to love and please Him.

That's the mainspring of our existence, and nothing in life works without it—not even Romans 8:28.

This is an observation frequently overlooked by the shallow and sentimental authors of most positive-thinking books. Over the years, I've read a lot of them, and there are a handful of motivational and self-help books that I greatly appreciate. I'm melancholic by nature, and I've suffered some depression. I've found that a shelf of uplifting books helps me keep my thoughts tilted positively, so I have quite a collection of volumes both religious and secular. But I don't recall even one of these books devoting as much as a single chapter to the primary requirement and condition necessary for claiming the optimism of Romans 8:28—loving God.

Yet this is the greatest of all the commands. Jesus Himself summarized all the requirements of the Old Testament by telling us to love God and to love people. When we genuinely fall in love with the Lord, we naturally keep His commands and do what pleases Him. That's why the Bible says that loving God is tantamount to fulfilling the Law.

The French mystic, François Fénelon wrote, "He who is in the state of pure or perfect love, has all the moral and Christian virtues in himself. If temperance, forbearance, chastity, truth, kindness, forgiveness, justice, may be regarded as virtues, there can be no doubt that they are all included in holy love. That is to say, the principle of love will not fail to develop itself in each of these forms. St. Augustine remarks that love is the foundation, source, or principle of all the virtues."

The Bible's Best Promises

As I searched this subject in the Bible, I was surprised—though I don't know why I should have been surprised—to discover the Bible reserves its best promises exclusively for those who love God.

A few miles from my house is a dam holding back the waters of Percy Priest Lake. The builders constructed a row of sluices or watergates that, when opened, release the waters of the lake into the Stones River. Think of all the promises and blessings of God as a vast lake whose bottom has never been fathomed and whose shores cannot be charted. From that boundless lake flows the River Blessing that constantly irrigates our lives. Psalm 36:8 says, "You give them drink from your river of delights" (NIV).

Loving God is the key that opens the sluices and releases the blessings. The floodgates open in direct proportion to our love for the Lord.

That's the constant drumbeat of Scripture. I want you to read the following verses. Don't merely scan them or skip over them. Take a moment to think through them, and as you read, notice the text I've emphasized. Notice how God attaches His greatest promises to the nonnegotiable condition of loving Him:

- "Know that Yahweh your God is God, the faithful God who keeps His gracious covenant loyalty for a thousand generations *with those who love Him* and keep His commands" (Deut. 7:9).
- "Turn to me and be gracious to me, as is Your practice toward *those who love Your name*" (Ps. 119:132).
- "The Lord guards all *those who love Him*" (Ps. 145:20a).
- Jesus answered, "*If anyone loves Me* . . . My Father will love him, and We will come to him and make Our home with him" (John 14:23).
- It is written: "What no eye has seen and no ear has heard, and what has never come into a man's heart, is what God has prepared *for those who love Him*" (1 Cor. 2:9).
- "*If anyone loves God,* he is known by Him" (1 Cor. 8:3).
- "Grace be with *all who have undying love for our Lord Jesus Christ*" (Eph. 6:24).
- "Blessed is a man who endures trials, because when he

passes the test he will receive the crown of life that He has promised *to those who love Him*" (James 1:12).
- "Listen, my dear brothers: Didn't God choose the poor in this world to be rich in faith and heirs of the kingdom that He has promised *to those who love Him?*" (James 2:5).

Those last words from James 2:5 summarize this concept: "the kingdom that He has promised to those who love Him." His richest promises are exclusively for God-lovers. This principle is stated in reverse in 1 Corinthians 16:22: "If anyone does not love the Lord, a curse be on him." Those who love God receive a never-ceasing cataract of eternal blessings; those who don't love God are left with nothing but a cursed life, even if they appear successful.

So God's promises are not distributed wholesale to every inhabitant on earth; they are the exclusive domain of those who love Him. It shouldn't surprise us, then, that God occasionally sticks a divine thermometer into our mouths to measure the temperature of our love for Him. Paul told the Corinthians that sometimes it's necessary to test the sincerity of our love (2 Cor. 8:8).

Have you ever had an experience in which God measured or verified your love for Him? I'm sure you have, and so have I. The Lord is a master teacher who gives periodic exams to His followers to see how they're doing in the most critical subjects. The scary thing is that sometimes we may not even recognize when God is testing us. Not only do we fail the test, we don't even know it's being given!

Here are some hints. Have you had a financial reversal? Have you had health issues? Have you experienced challenges in a treasured relationship? Have things been bumpy at work? Has a valued client changed firms? Has a longed-for goal vanished into thin air? Have your goals evaporated before your eyes despite intense efforts on your part?

Deuteronomy 13:3b says, "'The LORD your God is testing you to know whether you love the LORD your God with all your heart and all your soul.'"

Perhaps God is watching your reaction to see if your devotion to these things eclipses your heartfelt and burning devotion to Him. He's waiting to see if your all-encompassing love and trust in Him keeps your soul buoyant amid the passing concerns of life. I know a young man who is desperate to find a girl to marry, and he's gone from one to another without taking time to seek God's will. My prayer for him has been, *Lord, may he fall so in love with you that these girls will hardly even matter to him*. I'm praying that because I know that if he first seeks God and His righteousness, all these other things will come as a matter of course (Matt. 6:33).

It's our love for God that keeps the rest of our lives well regulated.

We have two dramatic examples of this in Scripture.

In Genesis 22, God tested Abraham's love by asking him to sacrifice Isaac, his only son whom he loved. Isaac was the longed-for son of Abraham's old age, the boy he had prayed about for many years. He was the light of Abraham's life, and we can visualize the old fellow kneeling over his sleeping son, stroking his hair, and loving him with all his heart. Young Isaac represented all of Abraham's hopes for the future. He was the promised lineage through whom the entire world would be blessed.

Abraham's love for his earthly son was so intense it could easily have crowded out his love for his heavenly Father. In one of the most unusual chapters of the Old Testament, God tested Abraham to see if perhaps his love for Isaac was greater than his love for the Lord.

Lest you think of the Lord as succumbing to petty jealousy, it's important to remember that it's love for God that aligns the rest of life in its proper groove. Our love for Him is the foundation for health and happiness in all our other relationships, and God wants to keep us well adjusted. When love for our Creator isn't the spinning core of our lives, we wobble like a spinning top that's off center. We're like tightrope walkers who go wobbly because the pole is unbalanced. We're like an engine badly in need of a tune-up.

The other great love test in the Bible is recorded in John 21, when, in the early morning sunshine on the shores of Galilee, Jesus subjected Peter to a painful series of examination questions, gauging the depths of the fisherman's love: "Simon, son of John, do you love Me more than these? . . . Simon, son of John, do you love Me? . . . Simon, son of John, do you love Me?" Peter was grieved that He asked him the third time, "Do you love Me?" He said, "Lord, You know everything! You know that I love You" (John 21:15b–17).

Previously Peter had failed the test, thrice denying the Lord. He had loved his own skin more than His Savior. Now, Jesus probed three times, asking, "Do you love Me? Do you love Me? Do you love Me?"

How would you answer Christ's question if He were looking into your eyes through the morning mist?

Our love for Christ is an inner commodity that grows stronger as the days and years pass. My wife and I occasionally share the story of our courtship and wedding. At the time, we weren't really sure we were in love. We'd never had many dating opportunities, because I was in school in Chicago and she was enrolled in college in South Carolina. There was no e-mail in those days, and no mobile phones. We had a lot of thirteen-cent dates (that was the cost of postage stamps in the early 1970s), and we had developed a great friendship. But we were frustrated by the miles between us, and I was too immature at the time to love anyone as sincerely as I should.

So I finally told her that if we were ever going to live near each other and spend time together and grow to love one another, we were going to have to get married. I bumbled through a proposal, and after a moment's hesitation, she accepted.

So we were married by faith, believing it was God's will and assuming that as we got to know one another better we'd grow increasingly in love. That's exactly what has happened. Thirty years have passed, and I'm more in love with her than ever. Sometimes I can hardly believe my good fortune in finding someone so perfectly suited to my personality, needs, and ministry. Our love, as the song says, is here to stay.

In the same way, our love for Jesus grows. We commit ourselves to Him like a husband and wife making their vows at the altar, and we learn the joy of living with Him each day, talking to Him in prayer, listening to His Word, worshiping Him, thanking Him for His blessings, trusting Him with our burdens, proving His faithfulness, and walking in His presence. We are called the "bride of Christ" and the "friends of God." In any marriage, the partners are either growing closer or further apart each day. The same is true for our relationship with Christ.

Test Questions

Would you like to take a self-checking examination to measure your love for God? The Bible gives us a series of "test questions," as it were. From my study of Scripture, I'd like to suggest we can gauge our love for God by honestly answering six questions:

1. Have I committed my life to Jesus Christ as my Savior and Lord?

- "I know you—that you have no love for God within you. I have come in My Father's name, yet you don't accept Me" (John 5:42–43a).

- "Jesus said to them, 'If God were your Father, you would love Me, because I came from God and I am here. For I didn't come on My own, but He sent Me'" (John 8:42).
- "Everyone who believes that Jesus is the Messiah has been born of God, and everyone who loves the parent also loves his child" (1 John 5:1).

2. Do I obey His Word in my daily life?

- "If you love Me, you will keep My commandments" (John 14:15).
- "The one who has My commands and keeps them is the one who loves Me" (John 14:21a).
- "For this is what love for God is: to keep His commands. Now His commands are not a burden" (1 John 5:3).
- "I am commanding you today to love the LORD your God, to walk in His ways, and to keep His commands, statutes, and ordinances, so that you may live and multiply, and the LORD your God may bless you in the land you are entering to possess" (Deut. 30:16).
- "Love the LORD your God, obey Him, and remain faithful to Him. For He is your life" (Deut. 30:20a).
- "But whoever keeps His word, truly in him the love of God is perfected" (1 John 2:5a).
- "And this is love: that we walk according to His commands" (2 John 6a).

3. Do I enjoy worshiping Him?

- "Let all who seek You rejoice and be glad in You;
  let those who love Your salvation continually say,
  'The LORD is great!'" (Ps. 40:16)

4. Is my lifestyle holy?

- "You who love the LORD, hate evil!" (Ps. 97:10a).
- "Do not love the world or the things that belong to the world. If anyone loves the world, love for the Father is not in him. Because everything that belongs to the world—the lust of the flesh, the lust of the eyes, and the pride in one's lifestyle—is not from the Father, but is from the world. And the world with its lust is passing away, but the one who does God's will remains forever" (1 John 2:15–17).

5. Do I radiate His joy?

- "Let all who take refuge in You rejoice;
  let them shout for joy forever.
  May You shelter them,
  and may those who love Your name boast about You."
  (Ps. 5:11)

6. How much do I really like other people?

- "If anyone says, 'I love God,' yet hates his brother, he is a liar. For the person who does not love his brother whom he has seen cannot love God whom he has not seen. And we have this command from Him: the one who loves God must also love his brother" (1 John 4:20–21).

How did you do?

It's frightening to think that love for God is a rare quality, even among churchgoers. Jesus lamented to the strong and vigorous church in the city of Ephesus: "But I have this against you: you have abandoned the love you had at first" (Rev. 2:4).

Jesus warned that in the latter days because of the lawlessness of the age and the breakdown of culture, the love of many would grow cold (Matt. 24:12).

Jude 21 warns us to keep ourselves in the love of God.

This is our supreme obligation in life. Jesus said the greatest commandment was to love God with all our heart, mind, soul, and strength. It's the summarization of the Ten Commandments and the encapsulation of all the Law. Our devotion to Christ isn't measured by our work for Him, our successes in life, our activities at church, or the pious nature of our image before others. It simply resides in a warm, all-encompassing, all-absorbing love and obedience toward Him whom we have not seen.

Is Jesus pleased by the entertainment you're viewing? The purchases you're making? The way you're honoring Him with your tithes and offerings? The thoughts that play out in your mind? The attitude you exhibit at work? The way you're loving your wife, honoring your husband, or respecting your parents? Is Jesus pleased with the frequency of your attendance at worship? Your intake of the Bible? The way you share your faith with others? The self-discipline and self-denial that keeps your life healthy?

Jesus said, "Whoever of you does not forsake all that he has cannot be My disciple" (Luke 14:33 NKJV). This doesn't mean that we renounce all that we have, sell all our possessions, liquidate all our assets, and, like St. Francis, leave family and friends to camp among the downtrodden and live a life of poverty. But it does mean that we are willing to do exactly that if God so calls us. It means that all we are and have is available to all that He desires and commands. As Major Ian Thomas put it, "All there is of God is available to the person who is available to all there is of God."[1]

I greatly admired the British evangelist Dr. Stephen Olford, who recently passed away after a lifetime of effective ministry. The last time I was with him, he was eighty-six years young, eager to train young preachers, appealing to me to bring young men to

---

1. Shared with me by a professor at Columbia International University who recalled hearing Major Thomas say these words in a sermon years ago.

his preaching seminars, and eager to discuss book ideas with me. Hearing of his death, I was greatly saddened, but it gave me a chance to reflect on his extraordinary life.

Olford was born to missionary parents and grew up in the heart of Africa. As a young man, he had moved to England to pursue a career in engineering. His college thesis was on the subject of carburetion, and he developed a special system he wanted to perfect. He took up motorcycle racing to do so, but on his way home one blustery night, he crashed and lay injured on the road in the rain for several hours. Pneumonia set in, and the doctors abandoned hope of saving him.

As he lay on his deathbed, Olford received a letter from his father in Africa. It had taken three months for the letter to make its way to England, and was written well before Stephen's accident. In the letter, Mr. Olford repeated an old rhyme: "Only one Life, 'Twill soon be past, / Only what is done for Christ will last."

Those words bored into the young man's heart like a laser. Slipping from bed, Stephen fell to his knees and prayed, "Lord, You have won and I own You as King of Kings and Lord of Lords . . . and Lord, if you will heal my body, I will serve you anywhere, anytime, and at any cost."

God did grant healing to Stephen Olford, and from that moment until the day he died, he was a firestorm of ministry, burning with love for Jesus Christ, willing to go anywhere, anytime, and at any cost if the Master but beckoned.[2]

The Bible says: "Here's what I want you to do, God helping you: Take your everyday, ordinary life—your sleeping, eating, going-to-work, and walking-around life—and place it before God as an offering. Embracing what God does for you is the best thing you can do for him" (Rom. 12:1 MSG).

---

2. Roger D. Willmore, "First Person: A Tribute to Stephen Olford," *BP News*, 3, September 2004, accessed on 7, September 2004 at www.bpnews.net/printerfriendly.asp?ID=19028.

Take a few moments to think about this. Is your heart ablaze with love for Jesus? Is the heat and light of that fire noticeable to others, even from a distance? Can you say:

> My Jesus, I love You; I know You are mine,
> For You all the follies of sin I resign?
> —William R. Featherston (1864)

If so, He says to you: "In return, I guarantee that everything in your life is going to work together for good, every day, come what may, without fail, world without end." That's the promise of Romans 8:28, and even its condition is a blessing.

> Once earthly joy I craved, sought peace and rest;
> Now Thee alone I seek, give what is best.
> This all my prayer shall be: More love, O Christ
>   to Thee;
> More love to Thee, more love to Thee!
> —Elizabeth P. Prentiss (1856)

CHAPTER 9

Who Are Called According to His Purpose

**We know that all things work together
for the good of those who love God:
those who are called according to His purpose.**

Recently I read the story of a Navy pilot named Porter Halyburton who was shot down over North Vietnam in October of 1965 and thrown into the dreaded POW camp known as the "Hanoi Hilton." He was a southern white boy who had always felt superior and prejudiced because of his skin color. At the Hanoi Hilton, he found himself in a cell with a black man named Fred Cherry, who had been shot down nine months earlier. At first, neither man liked or trusted the other. But Fred was in bad shape. His arm, shoulder, and ankle were all broken, and he had received no medical attention. He was feverish, his shoulder was infected, and the flesh around the wound was rotting.

Porter took a deep breath and started taking care of Fred. He forced him to eat. He bathed him and carried him to the waste bucket. Despite the awful odor from Fred's left shoulder, Porter cleaned his wounds and tended to him and carefully tucked him into bed each night. He helped him dress and bathe, and he helped Fred attend to whatever personal hygiene the men could manage amid the squalor and filth of their surroundings. Porter talked to Fred continually to keep his mind occupied, and in time the two men became closer than brothers.

Later Fred Cherry said that it was Porter Halyburton who saved his life, but Porter claimed it was the other way around. Caring for his buddy gave him a reason to live, a mission, and a cause that kept him going.[1]

Pity the person who has no purpose in life. A sense of purpose is necessary for a meaningful life; it's what keeps us going.

Well, God also has a sense of purpose, and our lives make sense only when they conform to the purpose of His will as revealed in Christ Jesus. The great promise of Romans 8:28 is connected with that very thing. Those who love God find themselves agreeing with and attaching themselves to His purpose. The last phrase of the verse says "who are called according to His purpose."

This is the most difficult part of Romans 8:28 to interpret, and it makes sense only when we go on and read the subsequent sentence in verse 29: "For those He foreknew He also predestined to be conformed to the image of His Son, so that He would be the firstborn among many brothers."

Verse 30 takes it a step further: "And those He predestined, He also called; and those He called, He also justified; and those He justified, He also glorified."

There's a sequence of logic here that reveals God's unfolding strategy for our lives, and in the next chapter, we'll zero in on the five steps of *foreknew, predestined, called, justified,* and *glorified.*

---

1. James S. Hirsch, *Two Souls Indivisible* (New York: Houghton Mifflin Company, 2004), passim.

For now, however, I want you to see the overarching theme. Remember that Romans 6–8 represent the S section of R.O.M.A.N.S. (see chap. 3)—the part of the book devoted to the theme of sanctification, the process by which we are set apart for Christ and grow to maturity in Him. One phrase in verse 29 summarizes this in precise and succinct form: "For those He foreknew He also predestined *to be conformed to the image of His Son.*"

God intends for His children to be conformed to the image of His Son. Verse 29 gives us the ultimate goal behind Romans 8:28, the purpose behind the promise. God, in His infinite wisdom and intimate care, turns everything that happens to us into tools for good, with a view toward molding us into the image of His Son.

The old word for this, coined by past generations of Christians but now nearly forgotten, is *Christlikeness.* That word represents the ultimate purpose of God for you and me. The Bible says that as we have borne the image of the man of dust (Adam), so we should bear the image of the heavenly Man—Christ (1 Cor. 15:49). We're to be transformed into His image from glory to glory (2 Cor. 3:18).

This doesn't mean that we will become omnipotent, omniscient, or omnipresent. We don't become like Christ in the sense of sharing what theologians sometimes call the noncommunicable attributes of God. We don't become superheroes who can walk around performing miracles on every street corner or reading everyone's mind. Jesus could do that, but I'm never going to be all-powerful or possess total knowledge. That's not what we mean by Christlikeness.

Nor does it mean we should wear robes and sandals and look like an artist's rendering of Jesus from an old Sunday school leaflet.

Christlikeness means that the character and attitudes of our Lord should increasingly be reflected in our lives, as a mirror reflects the image of a king or as the moon reflects the light of the sun. Someone put it this way: "God doesn't want us to become a god; He wants us to become godly."

That's His purpose.

Toward that end, He takes the tragedies, trials, and triumphs of life—all things—and uses them as classrooms in which we learn the great secrets of Christlikeness. He uses all the events of life as an arena in which to conform us into the image of the Son He loves.

I think the passage in the Bible that best describes "the image of His Son" is Galatians 5:22, which says: "But the fruit of the Spirit is love, joy, peace, patience, kindness, goodness, faith, gentleness, self-control."

Think of it like this. On some occasion when you're unexpectedly called on to lead a Bible study group or teach a Sunday school class, try this experiment. Hand out sheets of paper that are blank on both sides. On one side, ask the participants to list nine terms that describe them as individuals. "If you had to describe yourself using nine words or phrases," you might ask, "what would they be?"

How about:

Young	Tired
Above Average	Short-tempered
Successful	Busy
Kind	Broke
Winsome	

Now, turn the paper over and make a list of nine words that describe Jesus Christ. If you had to compile a list of nine qualities that summed up Jesus of Nazareth, what nine words would you chose? Galatians 5:22 gives us that list, a nine-point portrait of the personality and character of Jesus Christ.

Character of Jesus

1. *Love:* No one has ever loved the world as Jesus did. He loved the lovely and the unlovely, the upbeat and the downtrodden, and He loves you and me with an everlasting love. Everything He does is for our benefit.

2. *Joy:* Jesus was cheerful. His mood was strong and vigorous, and others felt strengthened in His presence. He appreciated the blessings of God and rejoiced in them each day.

3. *Peace:* He had a deep serenity at the core of His heart, and He never went to bed worried. He knew that all things—even His death on the cross—would work out for good.

4. *Patience:* Jesus had an internal gyroscope that kept His emotions balanced. He never overreacted. If He was angry, it was always measured, useful, healthy, and appropriate. He never lost His temper or spoke rashly.

5. *Kindness:* Every day, Jesus found opportunities of helping others. He scattered good deeds along His pathway the way the flower girl strews rose petals on the carpet runner at a wedding.

6. *Goodness:* Our Lord's heart never harbored an evil thought, and moral impurity never stained his mind. His thoughts, words, and actions were totally pure, morally good, and always beneficial.

7. *Faith:* The Father's abiding presence and unfailing promises saturated the mind of Christ like water soaking a sponge. Jesus was fully persuaded that God was faithful and that His Word was dependable. He had a confidence in life that never wavered.

8. *Gentleness:* Even when Jesus scolded the disciples for their unbelief or rebuked the Pharisees for their hypocrisy, He did so in a way designed to correct and heal. The downtrodden never felt uncomfortable in His presence. To the needy and simple, His touch, though as powerful as a lightning bolt, was gentle as a sparrow's feather.

9. *Self-control:* Jesus perfectly maintained the personal disciplines needed for holiness, health, and happiness. He was never controlled or manipulated by fickle feelings or rash desires.

These nine qualities perfectly summarize the personality of the Savior, yet they are called the fruit of the Spirit. Why is that? Because these are the attributes of Jesus Christ that the Holy Spirit wants to reproduce in you and me.

Let's go back to the lists you made in that Bible study group or Sunday school class—the double-sided page listing your description of yourself and of Christ. God's goal for your life is that the front and back of that paper be exactly the same. If you threw your page into the air, when it landed on the ground those nine words should be visible regardless of which side was up.

In other words, God intends to use all things in life as tools of the Holy Spirit to reproduce the image of Christ in us. It's not that we're to try to be like Christ; it's that the Holy Spirit replicates the very personality of Christ within us as we grow older and deeper in Christ.

Painting in the Louvre

Think of it this way. I love visiting the great art galleries of Paris, especially the Louvre and the Musée d'Orsay. Sometimes in these and other museums, I'll see an artist who has gained permission to set up his easel in front of a famous painting and copy it. Perhaps he is duplicating a Monet, for example.

But what if the very mind and spirit of Claude Monet could enter that man's body and fill his mind and take possession of his eyes and hands? What if, instead of imitating Monet, he could be filled with Monet's spirit so that the great Impressionist was really repainting his masterpiece through the hands of this amateur?

That's something of what Jesus Christ does for us by His Spirit. He indwells us, fills us, and clones His character and His life within us. That's why Paul wrote elsewhere in the book of Galatians: "I no longer live, but Christ lives in me" (2:20a).

The Christian life isn't merely a matter of trying to be like Christ. It's a matter of being surrendered to Christ, of being filled with His Spirit, and of allowing God the Father through God the Spirit to develop the very life of God the Son in and through us.

And according to Romans 8:28–29, the Father uses all the circumstances of life to bring about this good result. "We know that all things work together for the good of those who love God: those who are called according to His purpose. For those He fore-knew He also predestined to be conformed to the image of His Son. . . ."

But the verse doesn't stop there. It goes on to say: "For those He foreknew He also predestined to be conformed to the image of His Son, *so that He would be the firstborn among many brothers.*"

God wants to use all the circumstances of life to make us Christlike so that Jesus will be the great pattern—the first one or the firstborn or the master mold—for all the rest of us, and we, His followers, will be copies of Him—His brothers and sisters, His twins, His siblings who bear a family likeness. He is the elder brother and only-begotten Son who serves as the mold and model for all who are children of God.

The Phillips version of the New Testament puts it this way: "God, in His foreknowledge, chose them to bear the family likeness of His Son, that He might be the eldest of a family of many brothers."

Here's a real-life example. Jim Lauthern is a deacon in my church and one of my longtime friends. I knew Jim before I became his pastor, and I recall the terrible illness that struck him when he was forty years old. He was in the prime of life, and he and Shirley had three wonderful children. He loved his new job and he was active in his church. But almost overnight he landed in the ICU, hovering between life and death. He remained in the hospital for more than four months and had four major surgeries. A deep depression fell over him.

Jim had a friend, however, who sensed his depression and visited him every day. "Jim," said the friend, "the one thing you can do here while you're flat on your back is to develop a personal ministry of praying for others. I'll collect prayer requests and bring them to you every day."

That was thirty years ago, and, looking back, Jim told me, "During my illness God gave me a new ministry of intercession. I would not want to go through an illness like that again, but I would not trade the valuable lesson that the Lord taught me. I had been so busy I had never taken the time to be still and fellowship with God and pray for the needs of others."

One of the reasons Jim is such a valuable leader in our church is because of the maturing that occurred during his months of illness, which seasoned him for effective, Christlike service.

For the Christian, then, even sickness becomes a tool that conforms us to the image of Christ. That's why Charles Spurgeon, the great British preacher, quipped: "I dare say that the greatest earthly blessing that God can give to any of us is health, with the exception of sickness."

Or, as Thomas Watson put it, "A sick bed often teaches more than a sermon."[2]

I'm thankful to have been thus far spared from serious illness, but I've had other troubles in life. Without exception, the occasions when I've most grown spiritually have been the hardest periods in life. When I've faced an impending disaster, a run of bad news, a family crisis, a deep disappointment, a period of anxious waiting—those have been the days I've drawn closest to Christ, prayed the most earnestly, searched His Word the most diligently, and learned to trust Him in new ways and at deeper levels.

Recently a man in Houston told me of a harrowing experience he had faced. "I wouldn't ever want to go through that again," he said, "but I wouldn't give anything for having gone through it once."

The reason? He was thankful for all the lessons he learned, the wisdom he acquired, and the strength he developed while in the Refiner's fire. Now he's able to comfort others with the comfort he himself received from God (2 Cor. 1:4).

Missionary Amy Carmichael once wrote vividly of this. One day in India, she took her children to see a goldsmith refine gold after the ancient manner of the East. He was sitting at his little charcoal fire. Amid the glow of the flames he placed a common curved roof tile. Another tile was used to cover it as a lid, and this became his simple, homemade crucible.

Into the crucible the refiner placed ingredients: salt, tamarind fruit, and burned brick dust. Embedded within these ingredients was a golden nugget. The fire worked on the golden nugget, "eating it," as the refiner put it. From time to time, he would lift the gold out with tongs, let it cool, then rub it between his fingers. Then he would return it to the crucible and blow the fire hotter than it was before.

---

2. Thomas Watson, *Gleanings from Thomas Watson* (Morgan, PA: Soli Deo Gloria Publications, 1995), 55.

"It could not bear it so hot at first, but it can bear it now," he explained to the children. "What would have destroyed it then helps it now."

Finally Amy asked, "How do you know when the gold is purified?"

The refiner answered, "When I can see my face in it, then it is pure."[3]

The Lord wants us to reflect the image of Christ, and all things of life are sometimes the tools and tongs of the Refiner. He uses them wisely and redemptively. That's why every circumstance of life turns out for the good of those who love Jesus, and in the process He purifies us to reflect His face to others.

The apostle Peter wrote, "You have had to be distressed by various trials so that the genuineness of your faith—more valuable than gold, which perishes though refined by fire—may result in praise, glory, and honor at the revelation of Jesus Christ" (1 Pet. 1:6b–7).

Job said, "Yet He knows the way I have taken; when He has tested me, I will emerge as pure gold" (Job 23:10).

Without verse 29, Romans 8:28 is like a flower without its bloom. All things *do* work together for good—that's God's promise. But why and to what end?

Not merely for our happiness but for His honor—that Christ might be seen and glorified in us.

All things work together for good, not only to relieve our distress but to convey His glory and to uplift His name. God uses all things to purify, refine, and mature us, that we might reflect the character of Jesus Christ to a needy and darkened world. He wants to populate this planet with "Christ-ones"—Christians, twins of Christ who is, as it were, the eldest of many brothers and

---

3. Amy Carmichael, *Gold Cord* (Fort Washington, PA: Christian Literature Crusade, 1957), 69–70.

sisters, the brothers and sisters being those who love God and who are called according to His purpose.

So there's a divine purpose behind the promise of God's providence. As the hymnist put it long ago:

> When through fiery trials thy pathways shall lie,
> My grace, all sufficient, shall be thy supply;
> The flame shall not hurt thee; I only design
> Thy dross to consume, and thy gold to refine.
> —Attributed to John Keene (1787)

I have called Thee, "Abba, Father;"
I have set my heart on Thee:
Storms may howl, and clouds may gather,
All must work for good to me.
—Henry F. Lyte, 1824

CHAPTER 10

For Those He Foreknew . . .

In the devotional book *Voices of the Faithful*, a missionary couple in South America tells of a local pastor in Uberaba who bought a van to transport people to church. To help make payments on the van, he removed the backseats and did delivery work through the week. But the van needed four new tires, and the pastor had no way of paying for them.

One night the van was stolen from the church property. Some of the church members tried to console their pastor by saying that perhaps it wasn't God's will for him to have the van. But he knew he needed the vehicle for God's work, so he trusted the Lord to work it all for good.

A few days later, police officers from a nearby town called on him, saying the van had been located and the thief caught. Arriving at the police station, the pastor was surprised to find his vehicle sporting a new set of tires, new backseats, and a radio! He claimed the van, but told the police that the tires, seats, and radio were not his. They must have been installed by the thief.

"Well, I guess that is the thief's loss and your gain," replied the police officer. The pastor now has a good van, fully equipped and freshly shod.[1]

Good Luck?

Winston Churchill once observed, "You never can tell how bad luck may not after all turn out to be good luck."[2] But there's no such thing as luck for the child of God, and Christians shouldn't hope for good luck or bemoan when it goes bad. Luck is a worthless word. What we need is providence: God the Father, through the grace of God the Son and in answer to the prayers of God the Spirit, works all things for the good of those who love Him, in the process using the circumstances of life as arenas in which to conform us to the image of Christ.

If Romans chapter 8 ended with verse 28, we'd still be thrilled, but the chapter doesn't conclude there. There are still eleven wonderful verses to go, each one taking us higher and higher until we end the chapter in the stratospheres. Look at 28–30 again: "We know that all things work together for the good of those who love God: those who are called according to His purpose. For those He foreknew He also predestined to be conformed to the image of His Son, so that He would be the firstborn among many brothers. And those He predestined, He also called; and those He called, He also justified; and those He justified, He also glorified."

God wants us to see the machinery behind the mystery, so verses 29–30 explain that all things work together for good—not by whim or fancy or fate or luck but by divine decree. There is a chain of five golden links, forged from eternity past in the blacksmith's shop of the sovereignty of the eternal God, that anchors

---

1. *Voices of the Faithful,* Beth Moore, ed. (Nashville: Integrity Publishers, 2005; in conjunction with the International Mission Board of the Southern Baptist Convention), 233.
2. Quoted in *Reader's Digest World's Greatest Biographies,* 2001.

the promise of Romans 8:28. Notice the verbs Paul used, for they encompass the entire process of salvation: "For those He *foreknew* He also *predestined*. . . . And those He predestined, He also *called;* and those He called, He also *justified;* and those He justified, He also *glorified.*"

All these verbs are given in the past tense, as though they were already done. This opens to us a marvel and a mystery. God dwells in eternity. To Him, time is merely a flash of a moment in which His intentions are put on a human continuum. As far as He is concerned, the entire scope and sweep of His purpose in our lives was accomplished at the very moment it entered His infinite mind. In fact, since His mind is immeasurable and His essence is eternal, there presumably was never a time when we were not in His mind or on His heart. From eternity past, His purposes are established. That's why Paul used the past (Greek aorist) tense here.

Revelation 13:8 is another biblical example of this "prophetic past" tense. Here we learn that during the Great Tribulation (a period still in the future), multitudes of people will worship the Antichrist. These will be people whose names are not written in the book of "the Lamb that was slain from the creation of the world" (8b NIV).

Our Lord Jesus—the Lamb—was slain from the creation of the world. In other words, the eternal God, for whom time itself is but the twinkling of an eye, foreordained and predestined a plan of redemption before the world came into existence, and in the limitless and eternal mind of God, Christ was slain at that moment, long before the world began.

In other words, the moment God thought it, it was as good as done.

English professors have a certain form of verb they call the past infinitive. Well, speaking metaphorically, the verbs in Romans 8:29 and 30 are in a sort of past infinitive. In the fathomless eons of eternity past, God thought, He decided, and He spoke. And what He thought, decided, and spoke was as good as done. In that sense, Christ was slain from before the foundation of the world, and in that way we were foreknown, predestined, called, justified, and glorified before the world was created.

Let's look at these words one by one.

He Foreknew

Romans 8:29 says: "For those He foreknew . . . ." At the very least, foreknowledge is a subset of God's omniscience.[3] Because God is omniscient (having total knowledge), He possesses perfect and complete foreknowledge; He knows all things in advance. Even more, He has always intuitively and totally known all things, and, conceivably, there was never a time when God did not possess total knowledge of all things, both realities or potentials. As theologian Henry Thiessen put it: "By the omniscience of God we mean that He knows Himself and all other things, whether they be actual or merely possible, whether they be past, present, or future, and that He knows them perfectly and from all eternity. He knows things immediately, simultaneously, exhaustively, and truly."[4]

> **Isaiah 46:9b–11**
>
> God declared, "I am God, and there is no other; I am God, and no one is like Me. I declare the end from the beginning, and from long ago what is not yet done, saying: My plan will take place, and I will do My will. . . . I have spoken; so I will also bring it about. I have planned it; I will also do it."

---

3. Many interpreters believe the word "foreknew" in verse 29 goes beyond God's omniscience to include His omnipotence and His loving grace toward the redeemed. If so, the precise application here would be limited to God's chosen ones—Christians. While mentally God certainly does foreknow everything about everyone, there is a special sense in which He foreknows/foreordains His own. Charles Williams translation (*The New Testament in the Language of the People*) interprets foreknowledge in this way by rendering the verse like this: "For those on whom he set His heart beforehand He marked off as His own . . . and those whom He marked off as His own He also calls." Dr. Martyn Lloyd-Jones agrees with this interpretation, stating in his exposition of Romans 8 that there is very little difference between foreknowledge and predestination. This is debatable among scholars, and we don't have to settle those differences before appreciating Romans 8:29. It's enough to realize that God knew us long before we knew Him. We are foreknown in His omniscient mind from the foundation of the world.

4. Henry Clarence Thiessen, *Introductory Lectures in Systematic Theology* (Grand Rapids, MI: Eerdmans, 1949), 124.

According to Romans 8:29, God's omniscience extends to us. He knew and loved us from the endless ages of the infinite past. He knew you before there was a *you* to know. Before you were conceived in your mother's womb, God knew all about you. Before your parents or grandparents were born, God cared for you. Before Christ died on the cross, He knew and loved you. Before Adam and Eve were cocooned in the Garden of Eden, God knew you as well as He knows you now.

You have been foreknown from the beginning of time. God has always known in advance exactly what you would look like. He has always known your innermost thoughts, your background, your history, your problems, your struggles, your strengths, your weaknesses, and the course of your life. He has always known His plans for you. With a single glance He knew all about you, long before the earth launched its maiden orbit around the sun.

This was profound and praiseworthy to the psalmist. He exclaimed in Psalm 139:6a, "This extraordinary knowledge is beyond me."

It's beyond me, too, but it's wonderful.

He Predestined

Verse 29 goes on to say: "For those He foreknew He also predestined."

Before You Were Born

When God called the prophet Jeremiah, He told him, "Before I formed you in the womb, I knew you; before you were born I sanctified you; I ordained you a prophet to the nations" (Jer. 1:5 NKJV).

Isaiah 49:1b says, "'Before I was born the LORD called me; from my birth He has made mention of my name'" (NIV).

The apostle Paul said, "God . . . separated me from my mother's womb and called me through His grace" (Gal. 1:15 NKJV).

The psalmist said, "You were there while I was being formed in utter seclusion! You saw me before I was born and scheduled each day of my life before I began to breathe. Every day was recorded in your book" (Ps. 139:15–16 TLB).

This touches on one of the deepest mysteries of theology, and scholars endlessly debate the tension between divine sovereignty and human responsibility. It's not my purpose to address that issue, except to say that it seems to me the Bible teaches both truths. God is sovereign, but within His sovereignty and without diminishing it, He has allowed us a certain freedom of the will to make moral choices.

It reminds me of a story attributed to Charles Spurgeon. When someone asked him how he reconciled divine sovereignty with human responsibility, he shrugged and said, "Why should I try to reconcile friends?"

In his book *The Invisible Hand*, R. C. Sproul wrote something that helped me develop my thinking along these lines, pointing out the distinction between a mystery and a contradiction. A contradiction is defined by the classic rules of logic, in that the law of noncontradiction states that something cannot be what it is and not be what it is at the same time and in the same sense. A mystery, on the other hand, is something that is true but which we do not fully understand.[5]

To believe in both God's sovereignty and human responsibility is not illogical, because the tension between these two ideas does not constitute a contradiction but a mystery.

I don't understand exactly how the divine sovereignty and human responsibility work together, but I believe both are true. It's like the time in my childhood when my dad took me to the airport. We stood on the rooftop observation deck and watched planes take off. Even as I child, I understood the law of gravity, and I couldn't understand how those airplanes could defy it. When I asked my dad, he said something about the laws of aerodynamics. I didn't understand much about it, and the two laws appeared

---

5. R. C. Sproul, *The Invisible Hand* (Phillipsburg, NJ: P & R Publishing, 1996), 80–83.

to me to be contradictions. Actually they were mysteries, which, now that I'm older and better informed, make total sense.

Right now, I'm like a child looking at divine sovereignty and human responsibility and believing both are true and noncontradictory. But I don't yet have enough knowledge to fully understand how they come together. As I continue to study it more, I'm sure my understanding will develop, and in heaven, I expect to have a much better grasp of it. But it doesn't bother me to have mystery amid my Christian beliefs. Why would I want to worship a God I could totally figure out? Why would I want to serve a God who isn't transcendent? Mysterious? Awe-inspiring? Mind-boggling?

Some doctrines are so deep that I can only state them, accept them, rejoice in them, and study them as well as I can in Scripture, but I can't get to the bottom of them any more than I could jump out of a boat and swim to the bottom of the ocean.

That's how I feel about predestination. I don't fully understand it, but I read it in the Scriptures, can state it theologically, can rejoice in it, and can say, "Lord, thank You!"

How wonderful to know that God loves us with an everlasting love and that He has predestined us to be His children. Ephesians says, "He chose us in Him, before the foundation of the world. . . . He predestined us to be adopted through Jesus Christ for Himself . . . predestined according to the purpose of the One who works out everything in agreement with the decision of His will" (1:4–5, 11b).

He Called and Justified

Third, He called us. The New Testament frequently uses this term to describe that action of God by which He draws us to Himself in salvation. For example, at the beginning of this book of Romans, Paul described the Christians in Rome as those "who are also Jesus Christ's by calling . . . called as saints" (1:6–7).

In 1 Corinthians 1:9, he wrote, "God is faithful; by Him you were called into fellowship with His Son, Jesus Christ our Lord."

Hebrews 3:1a says that we are "holy brothers and companions in a heavenly calling."

Peter wrote, "But you are 'a chosen race, a royal priesthood, a holy nation, a people for His possession, so that you may proclaim the praises' of the One who called you out of darkness into His marvelous light" (1 Pet. 2:9).

And then He justified us. As we've seen, this is the great theme of the book of Romans. It means that God has taken our sins and transferred them to the account of His Son, and He has taken the righteous merits of Christ and credited or reckoned them to our account. When He looks at us, therefore, He does so through the prism of Jesus Christ, and we are righteous in His sight.

He Glorified

Fifth, He glorified us. This is the last stage of our salvation, and it's still in the future. When Christ comes again with a shout, with the voice of the archangel, and with the trumpet call of God, we'll be raised incorruptible. Out of the sea, out of the ground, out of the ashes, we'll arise. Graves will be emptied, and the earth will give up its dead in Christ. We'll be transformed in a moment, in the twinkling of an eye, and our bodies will become as ageless, deathless, and marvelous as the risen body of Christ when He emerged from the tomb on the first Easter.

Philippians 3:21 says, "He will transform the body of our humble condition into the likeness of His glorious body, by the power that enables Him to subject everything to Himself."

To be glorified means to be absolutely perfect, with an absolutely perfect God, in an absolutely perfect place, with an absolutely perfect body, endlessly and forever. When Jesus rose from the dead, He emerged from the tomb in His glorified state. His human body was transformed and equipped for eternity. The same thing will happen at the moment of our resurrection, and the last two chapters of the Bible describe our glorified state in the new heavens and on the new earth and in the New Jerusalem. Revelation 21 and 22 are simply a two-chapter explanation of this single word—*glorified*—in Romans 8:30.

As described in Revelation 21 and 22, heaven will be a place of unimagined beauty. Think of the most beautiful place you've ever visited. Maybe it was a national park or a quiet lake in the mountains. Perhaps it was a mountain summit and overview. Think of the loveliest boulevard down which you've ever strolled or the most gorgeous riverside walk you've ever enjoyed.

I'm grateful to have had the opportunity of traveling around the world, and sometimes I've been overwhelmed at the beauty of this living planet. If I had to pick the most beautiful spot on this world, I'm not sure what I would say. I've seen the Grand Canyon of Arizona and the Copper Canyon of Mexico. I've seen the mighty Iguaçu Falls of Brazil and the towering Alps of Austria and Switzerland. I've been to the Arctic Circle of Finland and to the Great Wall of China. I've flown over the vast wasteland of the Sahara Desert in North Africa and walked across the White Sands of New Mexico.

If I had to instantly name the most beautiful spot in the world, I think I would choose the national parks of California—Yosemite, Kings Canyon, and Sequoia. It's hard to imagine anywhere more beautiful than those parks—unless it's my own Tennessee mountains.

As I've gazed at these spots of beauty, I've often thought of the old gospel song "How Beautiful Heaven Must Be." If this sin-cursed, polluted, spoiled, aging world is so beautiful now, can you imagine the pristine beauty that will surround us throughout eternity when God re-creates the world without sin, death, decay, or the curse?

This was on Paul's mind as he wrote Romans 8, and it should be on our minds constantly. In our lives this is still in the future, but in God's mind, it's virtually done. John Stott, in his wonderful little book on Romans 5–8, wrote, "So certain is this final stage of glorification that it is even expressed as an aorist tense, as if it were past, like the other stages which are past. It is a so-called 'prophetic past.'"[6]

More Than Conquerors

Think back over what we've said about Romans 8. Notice how the currents of this chapter have been heading in this direction all along. This is really an underlying theme of the entire text:

Resurrection: He who raised Christ from the dead will also bring your mortal bodies to life through His Spirit who lives in you (v. 11b).

Glorification: We suffer with Him so that we may also be glorified with Him (v. 17b).

Anticipation: For I consider that the sufferings of this present time are not worth comparing with the glory that is going to be revealed to us. For the creation eagerly waits with anticipation for God's sons to be revealed. For the creation was subjected to futility—not willingly, but because of Him who subjected it—in the hope that the creation itself will also be set free from the bondage of corruption into the glorious freedom of God's children. For we know that the whole creation has been groaning together with labor pains until now. And not only that, but we ourselves who have the Spirit as the firstfruits— we also groan within ourselves, eagerly waiting for adoption, the redemption of our bodies (vv. 18–23).

6. John R. W. Stott, *Men Made New: An Exposition of Romans 5–8* (Downers Grove, IL: InterVarsity, 1966), 102.

This, then, is Paul's great point: From eternity past, God has already known, predestined, called, justified, and glorified His children. He has decreed it from the foundation of the world, and it's as good as done. In terms of earthly time, however, we're still awaiting the completion of the process. We ourselves are groaning, because we are heavenbound people amid the struggles of an earthbound life. So the Holy Spirit who lives within us and who will one day resurrect and glorify our human bodies, is praying for us according to God's will. And because He is praying for us according to the will of God, everything that happens between now and then will be for good in our lives and will advance the immutable purposes of the God who has known, predestined, called, justified, and glorified us from eternity past.

Nothing can alter the purposes of God in our lives. Nothing can possibly happen to us outside this theological framework; all things will work for our good in accordance with God's invincible will.

That makes Romans 8:28 an anchor for our souls, held in place by an unbreakable chain of five precious links forged in the fires of God's sovereign decrees. Romans 8:28 is the culminating promise in the tower of logic that comprises the simple but sublime theology of justification by grace through faith as presented by the apostle Paul in the book of Romans.

All that's left is our response to it. What, then, are we to say about these things? That's what we'll look at next.

THE PROMISE

I Asked the Lord

I asked the Lord that I might grow
In faith, and love, and every grace;
Might more of His salvation know,
And seek, more earnestly, His face.

'Twas He who taught me thus to pray,
And He, I trust, has answered prayer!
But it has been in such a way,
As almost drove me to despair.

I hoped that in some favored hour,
At once He'd answer my request;
And by His love's constraining pow'r,
Subdue my sins, and give me rest.

Instead of this, He made me feel
The hidden evils of my heart;
And let the angry pow'rs of hell
Assault my soul in every part.

Yea more, with His own hand He seemed
Intent to aggravate my woe;
Crossed all the fair designs I schemed,
Blasted my gourds, and laid me low.

Lord, why is this, I trembling cried,
Wilt thou pursue thy worm to death?
"'Tis in this way," the Lord replied,
"I answer prayer for grace and faith.

These inward trials I employ,
From self, and pride, to set thee free;
And break thy schemes of earthly joy,
That thou may'st find thy all in Me."
—John Newton, Author of "Amazing Grace"

For the Christian, every tragedy is
ultimately a blessing, or God is a liar.
—R. C. Sproul

CHAPTER 11

What Then Shall We Say to These Things?

I teach a small Bible study on alternating Wednesday nights, and recently, as I worked on this manuscript, I decided I'd talk about Romans 8:28 with my group. After explaining the context, we discussed the verse, and the thing that struck us was its utter simplicity. Though it's arguably the greatest and most comprehensive promise in all Scripture, though it's rooted in the most theologically precise book in the Bible, and though it's the capstone and climax of Paul's greatest articulation of the doctrine of justification, the simplicity of Romans 8:28 is stunning. It's made up of the plainest one-syllable words in the English language, words you'd see on the reading chart of any first-grade classroom.

We	The	Those
Know	Good	Who
That	Of	Are
All	Those	Called
Things	Who	To
Work	Love	His
For	God	

The only other words in the entire verse are *together* (three syllables), *according* (three syllables), and *purpose* (two syllables).

Yet, compressed into these twenty-three humble words are the greatest truths to be found anywhere within the Scriptures or among the stars.

- John Stott said, "Romans 8:28 is surely one of the best known texts in the Bible. On it, believers of every age and place have stayed their minds."
- Dr. Reuben A. Torrey wrote, "Romans 8:28 is a soft pillow for a tired heart."
- John MacArthur called it, "Perhaps the most glorious promise in all of the Bible."
- David Jeremiah wrote, "How wonderful it would be if all things worked together for good *without* our knowing it, provided we learn about it later. But to know *in advance* that all things work out for good is heart-stirring. It provides a rationale for optimism in life. When we lay hold of this truth, it calms us down, builds us up, and sends us on our way rejoicing."[1]

The significant thing about Romans 8:28, as I've said, is its context—that is, where it appears in the overall sweep of the book of Romans. Remember the acrostic formed by the word *Romans* in chapter 3? After telling us that all creation is *R*uined by sin (1:18–3:20), Paul summarizes God's *O*ffer of pardon and everlasting life (3:21–31). He proposes Abraham as the *M*odel of those justified through faith (4:1–25) and explains the great benefit of justification, which is *A*ccess by faith into all the blessings of grace (5:1–11). We have a *N*ew Adam through whom we reign in life—

---

1. Quotes are from clippings in my files.

one Christ Jesus (5:12–20), which leads to an ongoing process of *Sanctification*, as described in chapters 6–8. We died to sin (chap. 6), still struggle with temptation (chap. 7), but the victory of Christ is ours through the Holy Spirit (chap. 8).

Romans 8 tells us that the Holy Spirit subdues our flesh, reassures us we are God's children, guarantees our resurrection and glorious inheritance, and groans with us in prayer as we groan amid the pressures of life. God the Father hears and answers, and all things work together for our good as we're being transformed into the image of Christ.

The Grand Finale

All that's left now is the grand finale, and that's how chapter 8 draws to a close. The Lord asks us a question: "Well, now that I've explained all this to you, what do you think about it? What do you have to say to all this?" He wants to know our response to the things He has revealed to us.

Verse 31a asks: "What then are we to say about these things?"

How should we feel? What should our disposition be?

If justification is God's gift through Christ's mercy, and if the ultimate result is that everything works together for the good of those who love God, how, then, should we think, feel, and live? How should we react to our daily circumstances? What attitudes should steady our minds and sustain our hearts today? How should we feel upon waking each morning? What should we tell ourselves in the face of disappointment? Difficulty? Depression? Doubt? How should we encourage others?

Paul's concluding paragraph to Romans 1–8 (8:31b–39) is the most soaring, breathtaking poetry in all his writings. It's as if all the bells in all the cathedrals on earth are pealing at once.

"What then are we to say about these things?" he
    exclaims.
If God is for us, who is against us?
He did not even spare His own Son, but offered Him
    up for us all;
how will He not also with Him grant us everything?
Who can bring an accusation against God's elect?
God is the One who justifies.
Who is the one who condemns?
Christ Jesus is the One who died,
but even more, has been raised;
He also is at the right hand of God and intercedes for us.
Who can separate us from the love of Christ?
Can affliction or anguish or persecution or famine or
    nakedness or danger or sword?
As it is written:
"Because of You we are being put to death all day
    long;
we are counted as sheep to be slaughtered."
No, in all these things we are more than victorious
    through Him who loved us.
For I am persuaded that neither death nor life,
nor angels nor rulers,
nor things present, nor things to come, nor powers,
nor height, nor depth, nor any other created thing
will have the power to separate us
from the love of God that is in Christ Jesus our Lord!

Read those verses again. Read them aloud and with vigor.
Notice Paul's five unanswerable questions:

1. "If God is for us, who is against us?"
2. "How will He not also with Him grant us everything?"
3. "Who can bring an accusation against God's elect?"
4. "Who is the one who condemns?"
5. "Who can separate us from the love of Christ?"

Notice the power of the justified life: "God is the One who justifies. Who is the one who condemns?"

Notice the centrality of the cross and empty tomb: "Christ Jesus is the One who died, but even more, has been raised."

Notice the motive that propelled God to send His Son to Calvary for our redemption and that eternally guarantees the promise of Romans 8:28: "Who can separate us from the love of Christ? . . . through Him who loved us . . . the love of God that is in Christ Jesus our Lord!"

Notice the utter confidence this imparts to our hearts: "If God is for us, who is against us? . . . we are more than victorious . . . I am persuaded."

Notice who is watching over our lives day and night: "If God is for us . . . His own Son . . . God is the One who justifies . . . Christ Jesus is the One who died . . . He also is at the right hand of God and intercedes for us . . . the love of Christ . . . Him who loved us . . . the love of God that is in Christ Jesus our Lord."

Notice the cascading cadence of Paul's emphatic conclusion: "Neither death nor life, nor angels nor rulers, nor things present, nor things to come, nor powers, nor height, nor depth, nor any other created thing will have the power to separate us from the love of God."

Notice the words that conclude the chapter like the last pyrotechnic explosions over Lady Liberty: "in Christ Jesus our Lord!"

Learning It by Heart

As I pondered this afresh while preparing this chapter, I felt ashamed that I've never memorized these verses word for word. Oh, I could quote them with reasonable accuracy, but every word of God is pure. There's no passage that presents a greater personal philosophy of workable optimism than Romans 8:26–39, and there's no excuse for any of us being unable to quote it exactly, instantly, and confidently at a moment's notice.

When I was a college student, I had an occasion to talk with Ruth Bell Graham, the late wife of evangelist Billy Graham, and she emphasized the importance of Scripture memory. From childhood, she had stored God's Word in her heart; and this passage was one of her favorites.

Later when Billie Barrows, wife of longtime Graham associate Cliff Barrows, was diagnosed with cancer, Billy and Ruth Graham came calling, along with George Beverly Shea and his wife. Their lives and ministries had been deeply interwoven across the decades, and sitting by the fire, these old friends spent the afternoon reminiscing and speaking of God's faithfulness. At the piano, Bev Shea played hymn after hymn as they sang and fellowshipped together.

Late in the day, the conversation died down, and a feeling of poignancy and melancholy threatened the little gathering. Suddenly and quietly, Ruth began slowly quoting this concluding paragraph of Romans 8: "What then shall we say to these things? If God is for us, who can be against us? He who did not spare His own Son, but delivered Him up for us all, how shall He not with Him also freely give us all things? Who can separate us from the love of Christ?"

Also in the room that afternoon was the Barrows's daughter, Betty Ruth, who later told me, "When Aunt Ruth broke the silence by speaking those words, it was almost stunning to me. I knew the passage well, but I'd never before realized the depth of comfort and hope it offered."[2]

Let's all memorize this passage, beginning with Romans 8:28 and ending with that soul-resounding declaration of faith that explodes like the final burst of a Roman rocket in verses 38–39: "For I am persuaded that neither death nor life, nor angels nor rulers, nor things present, nor things to come, nor powers, nor height, nor depth, nor any other created thing will have the power to separate us from the love of God that is in Christ Jesus our Lord!"

* * *

Somewhere I heard of a great cathedral in Europe whose prized stained glass window was shattered in a winter's tempest. The sexton collected all the pieces and stored them away in a large box in the cathedral's crypt. Two years later, a famed artisan, passing through the area, heard of the accident and saw the boarded-up window. He took the box from storage, worked in secret, and skillfully reset every bit of colored glass into a design of his choice. On Easter Sunday, the window was unveiled. It was an image of the glorified Savior, far more stunning and beautiful than even the original window.

The Lord takes all the shards of our circumstances and uses them to form an image of Christ within us so we might reflect His character and rejoice in His goodness. It happens through the genius of divine foreknowledge, foreordination, justification, calling, and glorification, which summarizes for us the entire scope and sweep of salvation. He does it because He cares for you. He loves us freely and He loves you deeply.

If He went to the extremes of Calvary, willingly offering His only begotten Son, will He not also freely give us everything else

---

2. Used by permission based on a personal conversation with Betty Ruth Barrows Seera.

we'll ever need for life abundant and eternal? Will He not always work all things for our good?

If He has justified us, can anyone ever condemn or destroy us?

If He has acted, can anyone in heaven or earth thwart His purposes?

No! No one! Never!

That's why *all* things work together for good. That's why He freely gives us *all* things. And that's why in *all* things, we are more than conquerors through Him who loves us.

Who Shall the Lord's Elect Condemn?

Who shall the Lord's elect condemn?
'Tis God that justifies their souls;
And mercy, like a mighty stream,
O'er all their sins divinely rolls.

Who shall adjudge the saints to hell?
'Tis Christ that suffered in their stead;
And, the salvation to fulfill,
Behold Him rising from the dead!

He lives! He lives and sits above,
For ever interceding there:
Who shall divide us from His love?
Or what should tempt us to despair?

Shall persecution, or distress,
Famine, or sword, or nakedness?
He that hath loved us bears us through,
And makes us more than conquerors too.

Faith hath an overcoming power;
It triumphs in the dying hour:
Christ is our life, our joy, our hope,
Nor can we sink with such a prop.

Not all that men on earth can do,
Nor powers on high, nor powers below,
Shall cause His mercy to remove,
Or wean our hearts from Christ our love.

—Isaac Watts

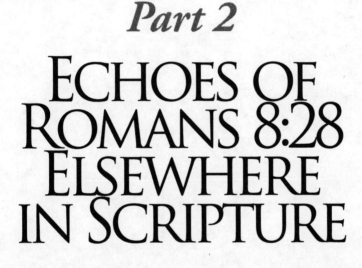

Part 2

ECHOES OF ROMANS 8:28 ELSEWHERE IN SCRIPTURE

*In him we were also chosen,
having been predestined according
to the plan of him who works out everything
in conformity with the purpose of his will.*
—Ephesians 1:11 NIV

CHAPTER 12

All Things Work Out in Conformity to the Will of God

Several years ago while speaking at Cedarville College in Ohio, I met a wonderful musician named Frank Fortunato. Frank was working with the missionary organization Operation Mobilization and for several years had directed the music ministries of *Logos,* an OM ship that sailed into various ports around the world to present the gospel and provide medical and humanitarian assistance.

Frank told me of an occasion when he was on furlough in the States. The *Logos* was sailing in Mediterranean waters, planning to dock in Istanbul, but the OM leaders didn't expect to stay there long. Turkey is a restricted-access country as far as the gospel is concerned, and the *Logos* crew expected Turkish officials to order the ship away as soon as they learned of the Christian nature of its mission. The *Logos* crew members prayed they might be able to stay at least forty-eight hours.

As the ship sailed into the harbor, the pilot gave the captain the wrong signal and the *Logos* collided with a ferry. Nothing like that had ever happened before with the *Logos*. The ship wasn't damaged, but the ferry sustained damage, and several people were thrown into the ocean. Everyone was rescued, but the Turkish police impounded the *Logos* until the courts could sort out what happened.

The missionaries, meanwhile, were free to roam around town. They offered to organize a concert for the city and were surprised when officials permitted it.

Ending his furlough, Frank flew to Istanbul to rejoin the *Logos,* unaware of these developments. While being driven from the airport, he was astonished to see his name blaring from huge banners. He couldn't read the Turkish writing, but he recognized his name.

"What do those banners say?" he asked his driver.

"It says that a Mr. Frank Fortunato is going to lead a citywide concert here the day after tomorrow."

Frank was flabbergasted, but he immediately went to work selecting a series of Christian songs and hymns designed to present the gospel. Each song explained an aspect of God's plan of salvation in logical sequence. At the concert and through subsequent contacts, large numbers of people were exposed to the Good News of Jesus.

And instead of being in Istanbul for two days as they had prayed, the missionary ship and its crew were there for one month, using every possible means to plant the gospel—all because of a dangerous collision at sea.

God choreographs all the events of our lives, and everywhere we turn, we can see Romans 8:28 in action.

In the same way, wherever we turn in Scripture, we can find this promise reiterated, repeated, and restated. There are echoes of

Romans 8:28 in virtually every one of the Bible's sixty-six books—the cross-references are too long to list. We also find the reality of this verse mirrored in story after story of Scripture.

Repetition is every teacher's best tool, and the Master Teacher uses it to our advantage, giving us statement after statement and case study after case study on this subject—how He takes our cares and concerns, turns them inside out, and by His grace uses them for our good.

To me, the most interesting Romans 8:28 cross-reference is found in Ephesians 1:11, and it's fascinating to compare these two quotes side by side.

Romans 8:28-29a, 30c

We know that all things work together for the good of those who love God: those who are called according to His purpose. For those He foreknew He also predestined to be conformed to the image of His Son . . . . He also glorified

Notice the parallels:

Ephesians 1:11, 12b

In him we were also chosen, having been predestined according to the plan of him who works out everything in conformity with the purpose of his will, . . . for the praise of his glory (NIV).

All things work together	He works out everything
Those He foreknew . . . He called	In him you were chosen
Conformed to the image of His Son	Conformity with the purpose of his will
He predestined	Having been predestined
According to His purpose	The purpose of his will
He also glorified	For the praise of his glory

In Romans 8:28, we're told that God works out everything for our good. In Ephesians 1:11, we learn that He works out everything in conformity with the purpose of His will.

Have you ever boarded a flight on an overcast day? From the ground, the clouds look dark and troubling, but a half hour after takeoff, how do they look? They're so blindingly glorious that sometimes we have to pull down the window shade. An airy carpet of burning clouds extends to the horizon, reflecting the brilliance of the sun and billowing into majestic shapes and sizes. Sometimes we gaze down on mountains, chasms, and canyons of dazzling vaporous forms, breathtaking in their beauty.

Romans 8:28 is a picture of how the promise of God looks below the clouds; Ephesians 1:11 is the same truth but from a higher perspective. Romans 8:28 is the view from the ground, as it were, and Ephesians 1:11 is how it's seen from heaven. Here on earth we see that everything works together for our good, but from a loftier perspective we see that everything works together for our good because all things work out in conformity with the purpose of His immutable will.

High Altitude

The loftiness of Ephesians 1:11 corresponds to the overall tone of Ephesians. In teaching through the book of Ephesians, I have sometimes suggested that we can understand Ephesians better if we'll take a moment to look at it through the eyes of Jude.

Jude wrote the next-to-the-last book in the Bible. As he opened his tiny book, he admitted that he badly wanted to write a book like Ephesians, but because of a crisis in the early church, he had to write a different kind of letter: "Dear friends, although I was eager to write you about our common salvation, I found it necessary to write and exhort you to contend for the faith that was delivered to the saints once for all" (v. 3).

In other words, Jude had wanted to write a letter about the wonders and glories of the salvation shared by all Christians, but because false teachers were threatening, he had to fire off a polemical tract about the dangers of heresy in the church.

Well, Paul wrote the book that Jude had wanted to write. Because the church in Ephesus was untroubled by division or doctrinal problems, Paul was able to write a book that, in essence, skimmed the cream off the top of his heart. He wrote about our common salvation, about our wealth in Christ, and about the wonders of God's plan for the church.

How Rich We Are!

Ephesians 1–3 describes the infinite riches of those who are seated with Christ in the heavenly places (2:6). Notice the recurring theme:

- "The riches of His grace" (1:7b).
- "The glorious riches of His inheritance" (1:18b).
- "But God, who is rich in mercy" (2:4a NKJV).
- "The immeasurable riches of His grace in His kindness to us in Christ Jesus" (2:7b).

Ephesians has been called the Mont Blanc of Scripture because of its soaring descriptions, thrilling insights, and lofty promises. When we read Ephesians, we're breathing the thin oxygen of high-altitude truth.

After the salutation in Ephesians 1:1–2, Paul took a deep breath and plunged into the longest sentence in the Greek New Testament. He started in verse 3 and didn't come up for air until he got to the end of verse 14. For the sake of simplicity, our English versions provide periods and pauses along the way, but in the original it's one rambling, run-on sentence. But what a sentence! Paul couldn't find a stopping place. He exploded with a torrent of theology and doctrine regarding our wealth, privilege, and blessing in Christ. Near the end of it, we come to verses 11 and 12: "In him we were chosen, having been predestined according to the plan of him who works out everything in conformity with the purpose of his will, in order that we, who were the first to hope in Christ, might be for the praise of his glory" (NIV).

This is so profound that it's hard to get our hands around it, but read the sentence again and notice how all the great truths are summarized in four words that begin with the letter *p*— predestined, plan, purpose, and praise. "In him we were chosen, having been *predestined* according to the *plan* of him who works out everything in conformity with the *purpose* of his will, in order that we, who were the first to hope in Christ, might be for the *praise* of his glory."

God Predestined Your Days

We've already come across this word *predestined* in Romans 8:29, so we don't have to be afraid of it. The Bible says that every word of God is pure (Prov. 30:5) and that we should live by every word that comes from the mouth of God (Matt. 4:4). So there's not a single word in the Bible that I want to avoid, but there are some that boggle my mind, and this is one of them.

Predestination means that we were chosen in advance to receive salvation. This theme dominates Paul's long introduction to Ephesians: "Praise be to the God and Father of our Lord Jesus Christ. . . . For he chose us in him before the creation of the world. . . . he predestined us. . . . In him we were chosen, having been predestined" (1:3–5, 11 NIV).

That word means God chose to save us from death and despair. From eternity past He determined to do whatever was necessary to release us from the slavery of sin and take us to heaven. He planned and predestined every detail. We were born at precisely the right time and in the right place, and everything about our lives has been thought through in advance. Psalm 139 says that every day of our lives was written in God's book before one of them began. God chose us to become heirs of God and coheirs of Christ.

That is a tremendously comforting truth that we can't do without. The reason it bothers some people is because they don't balance it with the parallel scriptural truth about human responsibility. As I said in an earlier chapter, the balance between predestination and free will represents, not a contradiction but a mystery.

On the one hand, the Bible teaches that God is sovereign and supreme and His decrees are infinite and absolute. On the other hand, it tells us to "choose this day whom we will serve," and that "whosoever will shall be saved."

The greatest minds in philosophy and theology have tackled this subject, writing innumerable books to explain how these two doctrines fit together, and no one has fully solved the dilemma.

My friend David Jeremiah recently put it very well when he said, "There are two tracks that run side by side from the beginning to the very end. One is the sovereignty of God and the other is the responsibility of man. Those two tracks never meet in this life. But like two railroad tracks that meet in infinity, when you look all the way down the road, you can see that they come together. And some day in eternity we will be able to resolve the issue of God's sovereignty and our responsibility."[1]

Those who stress human responsibility to the exclusion of God's sovereignty are robbing themselves of some of the greatest comforts of Scripture. To think that God has predestined my days, that He has planned my life in advance, that He has chosen me from before the creation of the world to be His child, that He is in control of all that happens, and that He is working out everything in conformity with the purpose of His will—what a truth and what an encouragement!

God Has a Plan

The second significant word in Ephesians 1:11 is *plan:* "In him we were chosen, having been predestined according to the plan of him . . . ."

While in college, I attended services for several Sundays at a particular church that didn't plan its worship services. Everyone gathered in a chapel and sat there, waiting for someone to get up and speak. If someone had an impulse to sing, he might rustle in

---

1. From a transcribed sermon by Dr. Jeremiah in my files; used by permission.

his chair, then stand and try to lead in a song. If someone had a testimony, she might fidget for a moment, then get up and share it. If someone decided to preach, he or she might do it. I didn't stay at that church very long, because the services left me feeling insecure and ill at ease. A certain amount of spontaneity is good, I suppose, but as a general rule I prefer forethought and wise planning.

If you don't think that God operates to plan, simply look at the universe. Before the stars were ever flung against the dark velvet of space, He had a design in His infinite mind. The cosmos is finely tuned and exactingly precise, and that's why earth is so perfectly equipped for life. Even after a century of hardcore atheistic evolutionary dogma, the American public and many, many scientists still reject the notion that the universe is chaos instead of cosmos. The evidence for intelligent design is overwhelming.

Look at salvation. Earlier in this chapter, I used the phrase, "the plan of salvation." It was designed in the heart of God before the creation of the world, and the moment that Adam and Eve sinned (as God knew in advance they would), the first promise of a coming Redeemer was given in embryonic form (Gen. 3:15). The prophecies and types of the Old Testament all pointed toward the Messiah whose life and work were preplanned in eternity.

Look at the Bible—sixty-six books written over fifteen hundred years by more than forty authors, and yet they all fit together like a masterpiece of literature with a common theme, a logical opening, a fitting conclusion, and an unfolding plot that centers on one great protagonist—the Lord Jesus Christ.

This same God who planned the cosmos, planned redemption, and planned the Bible also has a custom-tailored plan for you. The old Campus Crusade maxim was correct years ago when it said, "God loves you and has a wonderful plan for your life." Jeremiah 29:11 says, "'For I know the plans I have for you . . . plans for your welfare, not for disaster, to give you a future and a hope.'"

Paul asserted in Ephesians that in Christ we are chosen, having been predestined according to the plan of Him who works out everything in conformity to His will.

The Greek word translated "works out" is *energéō,* from which we get our English word energy. God's plan has the energy and the ability to work out everything as He intends—and it does say *everything.* Nothing is excluded. All our insurgencies, emergencies, and uncertainties. All things are worked *into* the plan of Him who *works out* everything according to the dictates of His purposes.

Like many students in my generation, I was greatly influenced by the writings of Dr. Francis Schaeffer. He was a brilliant missionary statesman, Christian apologist, and evangelist to the intellectuals, especially to young people of Western Europe who were seeking hope amid the growing fog of midcentury skepticism. Francis and Edith Schaeffer established a ministry in Switzerland known as L'Abri Fellowship, and it became a refuge and study center for young people seeking to understand the meaning of life.

The Schaeffers had gone to Switzerland as missionaries when Francis was thirty-six years old. At first they headquartered in Lausanne, but soon they moved into a chalet in Champéry, and there they entertained many American soldiers and European students searching for the truth.

But as their ministry was taking off, the Schaeffers encountered a series of unfortunate events. Their ministry split over theological issues, resulting in a dramatic reduction in their financial support. They also became the target of intense criticism because of their evangelical positions on various issues and found themselves in a firestorm of misunderstandings and confusion. Letters flew back and forth across the Atlantic as Francis Schaeffer tried to clarify his views.

Then another blow fell. Swiss officials decided to evict the Schaeffers from the country because of their success in winning people to Christ. Someone had objected to their work, and government authorities took the complaint seriously and forbade their living in Champéry.

In a relatively short period of time, the Schaeffers lost their denominational unity, much of their financial support, and their home. But out of this period of stressful uncertainty—indeed, because of it—a new ministry was born in a new place—L'Abri. A biography of Francis and Edith Schaeffer puts it this way: "Times were not easy. Satan attacked and buffeted them all along the way, but what Satan meant for evil God meant for good, and worked for their benefit."[2]

Put another way, everything happened according to the plan of Him who worked out everything in conformity with the purpose of His will. It is that way for all who love God and who are called according to His purpose, or as Ephesians 1:11 simply puts it, to all who are *in Christ.*

The Purpose of His Will

That brings us to our third word: *purpose.* "In him we were also chosen, having been predestined according to the plan of him who works out everything in conformity with the purpose of his will."

The preceding two verses explain God's purpose like this: "And he made known to us the mystery of his will according to his good pleasure, which he purposed in Christ, to be put into effect when the times will have reached their fulfillment—to bring all things in heaven and on earth together under one head, even Christ" (Eph. 1:9–10 NIV).

God's great purpose is that everything in time and eternity acknowledges Jesus Christ as Lord, and that the reign and rule of

2. L. G. Parkhurst Jr., *Francis & Edith Schaeffer* (Minneapolis: Bethany House, 1996), 88.

Christ be extended to the whole of creation, to the limits of infinity, and to the endless realms of eternity. The ultimate fulfillment of this is in Revelation 21 and 22, when heaven and earth are merged into the new heavens, the new earth, and the New Jerusalem. But even now, He is working out everything to conform to that result.

Joy Christofferson, a senior adult in my church, told me a story that bears this out. In 1951, her family was living in Chicago, and her mother was battling terminal cancer. The family was so distracted with caring for her that nobody bothered to put up any Christmas decorations when the holidays rolled around. As Joy's mother worsened, family members sent word to Paul, the wayward son, that he should come home.

Paul was the third child in the family. He had always been the mischievous one and had frequently been in trouble. During World War II, he had served in the Air Force as a nose gunner on a bomber and had earned a Purple Heart. After the war, he had turned to a life of agnosticism, adventure, and alcohol.

Paul's mother had written him about his need for the Lord, but his response was, "If you're going to write that stuff, don't write." So during her illness, she simply devoted herself to prayer on his behalf.

Now, receiving news of his mother's condition, Paul decided to see her. He had enough money for the bus fare, but severe weather hindered the trip. At one stop, Paul had to transfer buses, and in the process his luggage was lost. While trying to track down his belongings, Paul missed the outgoing bus. He had no money for a hotel room, so he spent the night walking the cold, dark streets of that city. He had plenty of time to ponder his life and the things his mother had written. Conviction seized him, and sometime during the wee hours of the night, he turned his life over to God and cried out to the Lord for mercy and forgiveness. Then he prayed specifically that God would let him get home in time to tell his mother of his decision to follow Christ.

Unknown to Paul, at the very moment he was praying, his mother was sitting in a chair as Joy bathed her feet. Suddenly the sick woman slumped over and appeared to have died. Joy yelled for her father. As they attended to her, thinking she was dead, she suddenly sat up, opened her eyes, and exclaimed, "It was so beautiful! It was so beautiful!"

Meanwhile, Paul's luggage was finally located, and he continued toward Chicago, but his trip was hindered again, this time by a severe snowstorm that stopped traffic for hours. Paul continued to pray, *Oh, God, let me get home before Mom dies.*

On Friday night, December 21, 1951, a knock sounded at the door. There Paul stood, travel-worn and anxious. Seeing his mother, he fell into her arms, and the two had a tearful reunion. He asked his mother's forgiveness and told her of his decision to let God take over his life.

The next morning, as Joy again washed her mother's feet, the dying woman muttered, "I'm thirsty." As Joy gave her a drink of water, she slipped away and went to be with Jesus. But it was all right now. Paul was home.

"What seemed to be a dark valley turned into a mountaintop experience," Joy told me. "The lost luggage, the snowstorm, the night of walking the frozen streets, the near death of my mother, the knock on the door, the reunion, my mother's flight to glory, Paul's conversion, his subsequent hunger for the Word of God— it was as though it were all wonderfully scripted by a divine author who was determined to finish the story with a happy ending."

That's the way the Lord works it out for all of us. Everything that happens to us—good or bad—is woven together into a fabric that honors and glorifies our Lord Jesus Christ—and that leads to praise.

PTL

And praise is how Ephesians 1:11–12 ends: "In him we were also chosen, having been predestined according to the plan of him who works out everything in conformity with the purpose of his will, in order that we, who were the first to hope in Christ, might be for the praise of his glory" (NIV).

Romans 8:28 tells us that God works all things in our lives for our good, and Ephesians 1:11 tells us that He works all things out for His glory.

The Lord wants the entire world to look at your life and mine and to glorify Him for the way He has worked on our behalf. He wants you and me to look at His handiwork in our own lives and to praise Him for how He has woven all the strands and threads into a pattern for His glory. He wants us to live a PTL life.

So, in the words of the German hymnist Paul Gerhardt: "Commit whatever grieves you into the gracious hands of Him who never leaves you, who Heaven and earth commands. . . . He will . . . find for you a way."

Commit Whatever Grieves You

Commit whatever grieves you
Into the gracious hands
Of Him Who never leaves you,
Who Heav'n and earth commands.
Who points the clouds their courses,
Whom winds and waves obey,
He will direct your footsteps
And find for you a way.

On Him place your reliance
If you would be secure;
His work you must consider
If yours is to endure.
According to His counsel
His plan He will pursue;
And what His wisdom chooses
His might will always do.

His hand is never shortened,
All things must serve His might;
His every act is blessing,
His path is purest light.
His work no one can hinder,
His purpose none can stay,
Since He to bless His children
Will always find a way.

Though all the powers of evil
The will of God oppose,
His purpose will not falter,
His pleasure onward goes.
Whatever our God decrees,
Whatever He intends,
Will always be accomplished
By the grace He sends.

—Paul Gerhardt

"You planned evil against me;
God planned it for good
to bring about the present result—
the survival of many people."
—Genesis 50:20

CHAPTER 13

All Things Work Out for the Good of Others

One of my favorite characters in American church history is Samuel Logan Brengle (1860–1936), a Methodist leader of the early Salvation Army movement whose writings on the subject of holiness are classics.

There's an interesting story about the way Brengle began his writing ministry. As a young, newly married man, he'd been placed in charge of a particularly difficult segment of the Salvation Army work in the slums of Boston. Across the street from his headquarters was a large and notorious saloon. One night as he returned home, Brengle discovered drunken toughs awaiting him, one of whom threw a paving brick his way. The man fired at close range, and the brick struck Brengle's head full force, smashing it against the doorpost.

For several days, Brengle hovered between life and death as his new wife prayed earnestly for him. When he showed signs of recovery, he was sent to a health resort in New York where he stayed six weeks. Returning home, he was unable to resume his schedule for a further period of eighteen months.

During this time he began writing out his thoughts and composing articles that were printed in the Salvation Army magazine *The War Cry.* These little columns were then collected into his first best-selling book, *Helps to Holiness,* which was published in a dozen different languages and sold record numbers of copies. It was the first of several wonderful little books that came from the heart and mind of Samuel Logan Brengle, and for the rest of his life wherever he went, he'd be stopped by people thanking him for his writings. His response was always the same: "Well, if there had been no little brick, there would have been no little book!"

One day, Brengle returned home to find his wife with the brick that had almost killed him. He asked what she was doing, and as she handed him the deadly missile, he saw that she had written on it the words of Genesis 50:20: "As for you, ye thought evil against me; but God meant it unto good, to bring to pass, as it is this day, to save much people alive" (KJV).[1]

That verse—Genesis 50:20—is the Old Testament counterpart to Romans 8:28. Prime Minister Joseph of Egypt spoke it after a lifetime of personal disasters and bitter disappointments.

The Bible devotes the final section of its first book (Gen. 37–50) to telling us this story. Why so much space? First, the Lord wanted us to know the significant elements of the early history of the Jewish people so we can trace the linage of the Messiah. Second, the Lord gave us Joseph as an early case study of the overruling power of Divine Providence for those who love God and who are called according to His purpose. Genesis 37–50 shows us that God can use an unfortunate series of life-crushing blows to bring about history-changing benefits.

---

1. Clarence W. Hall, *Samuel Logan Brengle: Portrait of a Prophet* (Atlanta: Salvation Army Supplies and Purchasing Dept., 1933), 88–90.

God is so good to do this and to do it so early in the Bible. It takes time to trace the providential care of God's sovereign oversight of our lives. In the middle of a crisis or difficulty, nothing makes sense. We have to look back at things from the perspective of elapsed time, like a motorist who finally makes it to the top of the mountain and then, from the overlooking bluff, can interpret the twists and turns in the road. It takes weeks, months, or years.

With Joseph, his life was an ongoing nightmare from the time he was seventeen until he was thirty, and it wasn't until many years later that the purposes of God became reasonably clear. Not till the last chapter of Genesis was he able to say to his brothers, "You meant it for evil, but God meant it for good."

In Genesis 37–50, the Lord collapsed Joseph's story like a telescope into about a dozen chapters of Scripture so we can sit down in fifteen or twenty minutes and read his life's history from beginning to end, and in the process we see the truth of Romans 8:28 exhibited in this abbreviated and inspired biography. God deliberately placed a gripping story of His providential control over the life of His children at the very beginning of the Bible to show us the wondrous truth that would later be articulated in Romans 8:28.

The Pasture

We can sum up Joseph's story using four words. Let's start with *pasture*. The story begins in Genesis 37:2–4: "At 17 years of age, Joseph tended sheep with his brothers . . . and he brought a bad report about them to their father. Now Israel [Jacob] loved Joseph more than his other sons because Joseph was a son born to him in his old age, and he made a robe of many colors for him. When his brothers saw that their father loved him more than all his brothers, they hated him and could not bring themselves to speak peaceably to him."

On the face of it, Joseph lived an idyllic life. He was a teenager with the coolest clothes. He had a loving and supportive dad. He had a good job, and his work gave him lots of time for solitude and kept him out of the mainstream of stress and tension. And from these chapters about him, we learn that Joseph was bright, responsible, imaginative, handsome, ambitious, and self-confident.

Sometimes everything seems to go wonderfully for us. We rise from bed each day and sing, "Oh, what a beautiful morning! Oh, what a beautiful day! I have a wonderful feeling everything's going my way." We should thank God for such tranquil and happy periods of life.

Yet things are never really idyllic on this earth. There were already stress fractures occurring around Joseph's life. For one thing, his father was showing favoritism and creating a destructive atmosphere in the home. Second, there were terrible blended-family problems here, with deep-seated antipathy among the stepsiblings.

None of us come from perfect environments. I loved my parents dearly, but they weren't perfect, nor have I been a perfect dad for my own kids. Every family has faults and failures, and those deficiencies can stay with us a long time.

Think of *your* background. What scars are left from your childhood or teen years? What habits and hurts have followed you into adulthood, like yelping dogs nipping at your cuffs? Can God use these things for good? Can He bring gladness out of dysfunction and wholeness out of regrets?

The answer is yes. That's one of the lessons Joseph teaches us.

But there was another problem here, and it was Joseph himself. As a teenager he came across as cocky and immature, which didn't help matters. He was handsome and muscular, and he seemed to know it. He was ambitious and he seemed to show it. He tattled on his brothers, flaunted his multicolored coat, and openly bragged about his dreams of grandeur. When it all blew up in his face like a self-made bomb, he had years of suffering during which to rue his own attitudes and immaturities.

That adds another layer to this story. Can God take our youthful immaturities and mistakes and turn them for our good later in life?

Yes, the story of Joseph tells us that God can bring good out of parental failure, family dysfunction, youthful immaturity, hateful attacks, and past mistakes—as we learn to love Him and respond to His call on our lives. When we take our situations, whatever they are, and place them under the redemptive blood of Christ, the sovereign workings of God's providence are activated so as to work all things together for good, conforming them to the purposes of His will. The Devil means it for evil, but God intends it for good.

The Pit

The next step for Joseph, however, was the pit. It happened one day when his dad sent him to check on his brothers herding flocks some distance away. The undercurrents of anger ran so deeply they were deadly. So when Joseph came to his brothers, they took advantage of their isolated location, stripped him of his clothing, and shoved him into the open mouth of an abandoned cistern or pit. They intended to murder him after lunch.

Nonchalantly, they sat down to eat. Suddenly, looking up, they saw a caravan coming from Gilead. A succession of camels was loaded with spices, balm, and myrrh, and the traders were en route to Egypt. An idea presented itself. "What do we gain if we kill our brother and cover up his blood?" said one of the brothers. "Come, let's sell him to the Ishmaelites" (Gen. 37:26b–27a).

One of the interesting things about Genesis 37 is that Joseph's reaction isn't given. What did he say? What did he do? How did he feel?

"Well," he told himself as he realized what was happening, "this doesn't seem like a very good thing, but I'm sure God will use it for good in my life. He's in control. No need to be too upset about being sold into a lifetime of abject slavery; in fact, I'm going to rejoice because all things will work together for my benefit."

No, he didn't say that. He wasn't experienced enough or sufficiently mature to react so calmly and with that much faith. In fact, Joseph was terrified and terrorized. He begged, cried, pleaded, and wept. His eyes were wild with pain, and he had to be subdued by his new masters.

How do we know? As the actual story is told in Genesis 37, we're only given the bare bones of Joseph's situation, not the internals of his responses. But later in the story, we find one verse that reveals his reaction. Years later, when the tables were turned and the treacherous brothers themselves faced possible imprisonment and slavery, here's what they said: "Surely we are being punished because of our brother. We saw how distressed he was when he pleaded with us for his life, but we would not listen" (Gen. 42:21a NIV).

The *Living Bible* says, "We saw his terror and anguish and heard his pleadings" (v. 21b).

We have another verse, too—Psalm 105:18—that gives further insight: "They hurt his feet with shackles; his neck was put in an iron collar."

Terror. Distress. Anguish. Pleadings. Shackles. One moment he was the favored son of a wealthy sheikh, a teenager with great dreams and idyllic ambitions, dressed in a multicolored coat of honor, stationed in the pastures of Canaan, watching his flock and planning his future. The next moment, he was torn from his family, ripped from his father's love, stripped of his ambitious dreams, robbed of his future, and lead away in shackles, wearing the loincloth of a slave.

One of the most frightening things about life is how quickly it can change, in an instant, in a moment. A phone call in the middle of the night. A police officer at your front door. A special news bulletin interrupting your TV comedy. A visit to your doctor.

It's easy to live in fear and anxiety all the time, because life is uncertain and the future is unknown.

That's where Genesis 50:20 kicks in: Though Joseph's brothers meant it for evil, God intended it for good. The Lord wasn't surprised by the turn of events, and He was determined to work all things together for good in Joseph's life for the benefit of others. In fact, these events that seemed to devastate were actually the tools God would use to protect Joseph's family, preserve the Jewish people, and safeguard the messianic line. Psalm 105:17 says that God sent Joseph ahead of them into Egypt.

The world and the Devil may spoil our comforts, our dreams, our wherewithal, and our apparent well-being. But they can't pry us from the invisible hand of God's constant care. Still, things sometimes get worse before they get better. Arriving in Egypt, Joseph was taken to the slave market. He was undoubtedly prodded, poked, and inspected by the traffickers in human flesh, and because he was so well-toned, handsome, and intelligent, he was purchased by a high governmental official named Potiphar.

About this time a very interesting phrase begins showing up in the text. If you read the story carefully, you can't miss it: "But the LORD was with Joseph. . . . But the LORD was with Joseph."

Genesis 39:2–4, for example, says, "The LORD was with Joseph, and he became a successful man, serving in the household of his Egyptian master. When his master saw that the LORD was with him and that the LORD made everything he did successful, Joseph found favor in his master's sight and became his personal attendant. Potiphar also put him in charge of his household and placed all that he owned under his authority."

But when it appeared that Joseph's string of heartaches was lessening and his situation was stabilizing, he faced another nightmare.

> Now Joseph was well-built and handsome. After some time his master's wife looked longingly at Joseph and said, "Sleep with me."
> But he refused and said . . ., "How could I do such a great evil and sin against God?"
> Although she spoke to Joseph day after day, he refused to go to bed with her. Now one day he went into the house to do his work, and none of the household servants was there. She grabbed him by his garment and said, "Sleep with me!" But leaving his garment in her hand, he escaped and ran outside. (Gen. 39:6b–12)

Spurned, the woman screamed, "Rape!" and accused Joseph of sexual assault.

The Prison

Joseph decided it was better to lose his cloak than his character, but it was a costly decision. Recently I read of a man who testified before a Texas State Senate committee about a similar experience. He was convicted of rape and spent seventeen years in prison before DNA evidence exonerated him. It's hard to conceive of being caught in that kind of horror, but that's what happened to Joseph.

And it was an Egyptian prison, to boot. Even today, the prisons in Egypt are reportedly among the worst in the world, with a reputation of being degrading, filthy, inhumane, and cruel. Think of what they must have been like more than three thousand years ago. It wasn't merely an overnight stay. Here Joseph spent the remainder of his teen years and the entire decade of his twenties.

Yet God was not inactive, nor sleeping, nor had He forgotten His young friend. He was watching over him, maturing him, working behind the scenes, and orchestrating circumstances. One night as Joseph tossed in his prison bunk, Pharaoh had a nightmare at the royal palace. It was so vivid he sensed it was a dream from God. He didn't know how to interpret it, but someone remembered that a thirty-year-old prisoner named Joseph was good with dreams.

Joseph, summoned and urgently needed, was quickly hustled from his cell, bathed, shaved, and dressed. An hour later, he found himself counseling the most powerful political leader on earth.

The Palace

By correctly interpreting Pharaoh's dream, Joseph made a powerful impression on the king of Egypt. He was instantly elevated to the office of prime minister, and within hours, the slave boy rose to the highest office of the land. "So Pharaoh said to Joseph, 'Since God has made all this known to you, there is no one as intelligent and wise as you. You will be over my house, and all my people will obey your commands. Only with regard to the throne will I be greater than you.' Pharaoh also said to Joseph, 'See, I am placing you over all the land of Egypt.' Pharaoh removed his signet ring from his hand and put it on Joseph's hand, clothed him with fine linen garments, and placed a gold chain around his neck. . . . And Joseph went throughout the land of Egypt" (Gen. 41:39–42, 45b).

It's hard to read the rest of the story without weeping, especially when we see how God used a famine to bring Joseph's brothers before him at last. Though they didn't recognize him, he knew them instantly, wept copiously, and then devised a little subterfuge of his own that brought them to heartfelt repentance and led to a joyous reunion with his old father, Jacob.

Jacob, remember, was the one who had moaned in Genesis 42:36, that all things were against him. In hindsight, we can say, "No, Jacob, it only *seemed* that way. All these things that appeared to be against you were used by God for the saving of your family."

Under the wise administration of Joseph, Egypt was saved from famine, the Hebrew people were saved from starvation, his father's house were spared from drought, the Jewish people were placed in an incubator where they would multiply into a great nation, and the messianic seed was preserved and protected as it wended its way through the generations toward the ultimate birth of the Savior of the world.

In his book on the providence of God, R. C. Sproul pointed out how all of human and divine history was changed by the simple gesture of Jacob giving Joseph a multicolored coat. If there had been no coat, there would have been less envy among the brothers. There would have therefore been no selling of Joseph to the Midianite traders. There would have been no journey to Egypt. No Potiphar. No Potiphar's wife. No prison. No meeting with the cupbearer and baker. No meeting with Pharaoh. And Joseph would never have become prime minister.

If Joseph had never become prime minister, the Jews would never have settled in the land of Goshen. There would have been no enslavement of the tribes of Israel. No Moses. No Exodus.

Without the Exodus, there would have been no Law given at Mount Sinai, no subsequent story of redemption, no unfolding of the history of Jesus Christ as we know it.[2]

But Jacob *did* give Joseph a specially woven coat, and God was in the details.

Of course, as Sproul pointed out, the Lord never leaves Himself without the necessary ways and means of accomplishing His

---

2. R. C. Sproul, *The Invisible Hand* (Phillipsburg, NJ: P & R Publishing, 1996), 95.

eternal decrees. The point is that even the smallest details of our lives—the inconveniences, the trials and tribulations, the suffering, and struggles—become nothing more nor less than ingredients in the cake of God's providence.

In other words, Joseph went from the pasture to the pit, from the pit to the prison, and from the prison to the palace—and every step along the way God was with him, causing all things to work together for good under the omnipotent hand and omniscient mind of His sovereignty.

The words *sovereign* and *sovereignty* are great terms in the Bible. They occur 305 times in Scripture. The prefix *sov* means "over," and the stem *reign* means "to rule from the throne." When we speak of God's sovereignty, we mean that He rules and reigns from His throne, and He rules and He reigns over all.

A young man recently said to me, "I've been reading about the subject of the sovereignty of God, and it's changed my life. It is the most liberating and empowering truth I've ever found in my Bible study."

A firm understanding and belief in the sovereignty of God relieves the mind of much darkness and heaviness. Dr. Martyn Lloyd-Jones, in his wonderful book on Romans 8, wrote about how inappropriate it is for Christians to be in despair or to sink in depression. He said, "Any Christian who is unhappy because of suffering, or who is guilty of any of the things I have mentioned under my negative headings, is found in such a condition for one reason only, namely, that he has not been thinking clearly. . . . [He] has not grasped the doctrines."[3]

Most people today have little use for theology and doctrine, but there's not a more comforting, bracing, or beneficial thing in all the world than discovering the doctrines and the truths of the

---

3. David Martyn Lloyd-Jones, *Romans: The Final Perseverance of the Saints: Expositions of Chapters 8:17–39* (Grand Rapids, MI: Zondervan, 1975), 24.

sovereignty of God, ruling and overruling the lives of His children, as a part of our inheritance and blessing in Christ Jesus our Lord.

Think of all the elements God threaded into Joseph's story—coats, dreams, parental failure, sibling rivalry, hatred, and immaturity. Even domestic violence, assault, kidnapping, and forced slavery. Caravans appeared at exactly the right time, and false accusations were leveled at the worst possible time.

Yet none of these things was wasted, and all of it was used for good and for the saving of many lives.

Now, what are your problems today? What's in your background? Who's in your way? What failures are dogging your step? The world may mean it for evil, and the Devil may want to harm you, but God intends to use it for good.

Another young man, a youthful German pastor named Joachim Neander, put it this way many years ago:

> Praise ye the Lord, who o'er all things so wondrously
>   reigneth,
> Shelters thee under His wings, yes, so gently
>   sustaineth!
> Hast thou not seen how thy desires e'er have been
> Granted in what He ordaineth?

*Indeed, it was for my own welfare
that I had such great bitterness.*
—Isaiah 38:17a

CHAPTER 14

All Things Work Out for the Deepening of the Soul

Whatever we thought of his policies, most Americans envied Ronald Reagan's sunny, optimistic view of life. *It's morning in America—Honey, I forgot to duck—Win one for the Gipper—A shining city on a hill.* This was his life's philosophy and the secret of the resilience and cheerfulness that sustained Reagan through an assassination attempt, a hostile press, a bruising career, and a turbulent presidency.

Where did he acquire such positive energy? Peggy Noonan, in her biography of Reagan, *When Character Was King,* claimed it came from his mother—and from his mother's Bible.

Nell Christian Reagan "was a Christian from the evangelical school and pretty much her whole life was bringing the good news to people who hadn't heard it or maybe hadn't listened hard enough." Nell had absorbed that classic book *The Christian's Secret of a Happy Life* by Hannah Whitall Smith, the theme of which is that God will let little befall you that will not be to the ultimate benefit of your soul. Nell Reagan believed that whatever happens to God's children will be used for good in their lives. That was her unshakable perspective.

Noonan gave an example in her book. After Ronald Reagan graduated from a Christian college in northern Illinois, he started looking for a job, but this was during the Great Depression, and jobs were hard to find. He hitchhiked to Chicago but had no luck. Returning home, he heard that Montgomery Ward was opening a big store in his hometown of Dixon, Illinois, and was looking for someone to run the sports department. Reagan, twenty-two, was the perfect candidate. He was a well-known swimmer and life-guard, and had been a football star at nearby Eureka College. The Montgomery Ward job paid $12.50 a week, and Reagan applied for it. Unexpectedly, the company passed over him and hired another local sports star. A disappointed Ronald Reagan shared his frustration with his mother.

She told him that all things were part of God's plan, even the most disheartening setbacks. If something went wrong, he shouldn't grow discouraged or feel down in the dumps. He should trust God with it and keep going. She told him that later on, something good would happen and he'd find himself thinking, *If I hadn't had that problem back then, then this better thing wouldn't have happened to me.*

Reagan believed it, every word of it, wrote Noonan. After all, it came from his mother's Bible.

Sure enough, about that time a local radio station hired him for $75 a week to broadcast sports. His name and distinctive voice became known throughout the Midwest. It was the first step on a path that was to lead him to become the Great Communicator in broadcasting and movies, then in politics, and eventually at 1600 Pennsylvania Avenue in Washington, D.C.[1]

---

1. Peggy Noonan, *When Character Was King: A Story of Ronald Reagan* (New York: Viking, 2001), 20.

What if Reagan had been hired at Montgomery Ward? What if his desires had been granted? The world would never have heard his name. But because of disappointment, he went on to change American history.

Isaiah 38:17a

Here's the way it's stated in other translations:

- "Surely it was for my benefit that I suffered such anguish" (NIV).
- "Indeed it was for my own peace that I had great bitterness" (NKJV).
- "It was for my own good that I had such troubles" (NCV).
- "See, this great bitterness was for my own peace" (Berkley).
- "It was for my own good that I had such hard times" (CEV).
- "Yes, now I see it all—it was good for me to undergo this bitterness" (TLB).

Another statesman learned a similar lesson long ago. His name was Hezekiah, king of Judah, and I'd like to show you a statement he made that fits perfectly the theme of this book. In Isaiah 38:17, he said, "Indeed, it was for my own welfare that I had such great bitterness."

Revival!

Hezekiah was one of the greatest kings of antiquity. His story is so important it's given to us three times in the Bible. Once in 2 Kings, once in 2 Chronicles, and once in the middle of the book of the prophet Isaiah.

He was twenty-five years old when he became king, and from the beginning he sought to revive the spiritual life of the nation of Judah. In the first month of the first year of his reign, he launched repairs on Jerusalem's great temple, which had become rundown and boarded-up. He tore down idolatrous images that filled the land and reinstated the temple worship of Jehovah. He called his nation to repentance. He reinstituted the Feast of the Passover, and a great spiritual momentum took hold in Judah. There was a quickening of the religious life of the nation, and the people of Israel turned back to the goodness, grace, and glory of God.

We long for such a revival today. Outside Lexington, Kentucky, is the little community of Cane Ridge. One day, about the year 1800, a man came to Cane Ridge to pastor three frontier Presbyterian churches. His fiery preaching started a spiritual awakening in that area, and as the churches planned their annual Communion service, they decided to invite other local Presbyterian and Methodist churches to participate. The revival spread, and the people planned a larger Communion service for the whole area the following summer.

To their amazement, hundreds and then thousands of people came in wagons, on horseback and by foot. For seven days, uncountable multitudes descended on little Cane Ridge as one preacher after another took to the stage to preach the gospel. Some historians claim that twenty-five thousand people showed up, and vast numbers were converted to Christ. It was a spark that set the nation ablaze in a revival that changed the culture of America. Though the Cane Ridge Revival is ignored by modern secular textbooks, it was instrumental in changing the trends of society for the next hundred years.

Wouldn't it be wonderful to have a revival like that in our own day? Revivals usually come when the times are darkest and the morals of a society are lowest. That's what happened in the days of Hezekiah. Under the preaching of Isaiah the prophet and because of the leadership of Hezekiah the king, a grand revival spread across the land. It can happen again as we pray as the psalmist did: "Will You not revive us again so that Your people may rejoice in You?" (Ps. 85:6).

Double Trouble

The Devil, who opposes spiritual revival on general principle, decided to strike back at Hezekiah's revival by attacking its leader; and suddenly, in the middle of everything, when Hezekiah was at the prime of his powers, at the peak of his manhood, and at the pinnacle of his usefulness, he was struck by twin disasters. It was a diabolical one-two punch, designed to spin Hezekiah to one side before snapping him to the other, a deadly duo of unfortunate circumstances. One was a military panic and the other was a medical alarm.

The military attack involved the invading armies of King Sennacherib of Assyria. Isaiah 36 begins: "In the fourteenth year of King Hezekiah, Sennacherib king of Assyria advanced against all the fortified cities of Judah and captured them." The mighty Assyrian empire towered over tiny Judah, and Hezekiah's nation was helpless to resist the invasion.

The interesting thing to me is Hezekiah's age. He became king when he was twenty-five; he had been on the throne fourteen years, so he would have been thirty-nine years old. Keep that in mind as you read this because two chapters later the other bomb goes off. Isaiah 38 begins: "In those days Hezekiah became terminally ill. The prophet Isaiah son of Amoz came and said to him . . . 'Put your affairs in order, for you are about to die; you will not recover.'"

I remember when my friend Jonathan Thigpen, who was my age, told me that his neurologist informed him he had a terrible, terminal illness, Lou Gehrig's disease, from which he eventually died. Jonathan said that as he left the doctor's office, he felt as if a dark and heavy blanket fell across his head, shutting out the light and leaving him suffocating in gloom and terror. In Jonathan's case, Psalm 46 came instantly to mind with such power that he was able to escape the despair. But it's hard to imagine getting the kind of news that Jonathan and Hezekiah absorbed.

Hezekiah wept bitterly, moaning, "In the prime of my life must I go through the gates of death and be robbed of the rest of my years?" (Isa. 38:10 NIV).

For the sake of establishing a chronology, let's fast-forward the story. In the end, God gave Hezekiah an additional fifteen years of life. Hezekiah was twenty-five years old when he became king and he reigned twenty-nine years, so he died at age fifty-four. If his life had been extended by fifteen years, how old was he when this sickness struck him? Thirty-nine.

Thirty-nine was a very bad year for Hezekiah. At the very moment he faced the greatest challenge of his professional life, he was stuck by the greatest challenge in his personal life. As king, he was facing a mortal enemy invading his land; simultaneously, as a man, he was facing his own mortality.

Sometimes problems come in twos and threes. We even have an entire set of terms to describe it. We talk about:

- The one-two punch
- The double whammy
- The double-edged sword
- Double trouble
- Fighting a war on two fronts
- Waiting for the other shoe to drop
- Going down for the third time

Consider the story of Phyllis Rutledge whose husband, Howard, was a pilot in Vietnam. On November 28, 1965, a Navy chaplain informed her Howard was missing in action. Not long afterward, her mother suffered a stroke and died. The next year as Phyllis vacationed with her children, trying to maintain some normalcy and sanity, her fifteen-year-old son, John, dove into the water and struck his head on a rock. He was paralyzed from the neck down. Triple disasters in a short period of time. Merely random accidents?

As I wrote this chapter, I received a message regarding my

friend missionary Janice Banks. Last month her husband was killed in a car wreck, and this week her mother passed away. A coincidence?

When we have sudden, unexpected problems on multiple fronts, they may represent a strategic attack by the Devil. That's one of the lessons from the early chapters of the book of Job, when Satan arranged for successive waves of tragedy to hit Job, one after another, in an intense, sustained effort to destroy his faith. These were Satan's cluster bombs. Remember that he tempted Jesus three times, one attempt after another in rapid succession. Whenever I see a series of unfortunate events occurring in my life, one after the other, almost in timed precision, I consider the possibility that this is a sustained, strategic satanic attack.

It is during these times that God wants to teach us His richest and deepest lessons: the Lord intends to stabilize, strengthen, and develop us—that's one of the reasons He allows troubles to come. They are His tools in conforming us into the image of Christ. That's precisely what happened with Hezekiah, too, and he later testified, "Indeed, it was for my own welfare that I had such great bitterness; but Your love has delivered me" (Isa. 38:17a). Hezekiah came through his experiences to teach us four lessons.

Prayer Really Works

The first lesson is: Prayer really works. Hezekiah met both his challenges head-on with the powerful missile of prayer. In Isaiah 37, as enemy forces flooded the land like water from a broken dam, Hezekiah went to his knees in prayer, and he sent out an urgent request for others to do the same. The message to the prophet Isaiah said, "This day is a day of distress and rebuke and disgrace, as when children come to the point of birth and there is no strength to deliver them. . . . Therefore pray for the remnant that still survives" (Isa. 37:3–4 NIV).

Therefore pray! Underline those words in Isaiah 37:4, for they represent our greatest strategy in the face of overwhelming difficulty.

Hezekiah then received another, more insistent communication from Sennacherib, this time by letter. It was a hostile, threatening document warning of doom and disaster if Judah tried to resist the Assyrian forces.

Have you ever received a letter, a bill, an e-mail, a summons, a medical report, or any other kind of bad news? I have, and it ties my stomach in knots and affects me physically. But from the example of Hezekiah, we learn one of the most powerful prayer techniques in the entire Bible. "Hezekiah took the letter from the messengers, read it, then went up to the LORD's house and spread it out before the LORD. Hezekiah prayed to the LORD" (Isa. 37:14–15).

We can often do the same thing literally, and we can always do it figuratively. Try taking those unpaid bills to your bedside, getting down on your knees, and spreading them out before the Lord. Take that newspaper headline that worries you, go to your altar, wherever it is, and spread it out before the Lord. Take that missionary letter and do the same. Take a picture of your loved one about whom you're concerned. Take the map showing the location of your loved one in the armed forces. Take your medical report, your credit rating, your child's report card, or the critical letter you received. Spread it out before the Lord as a way of entrusting it to Him.

The Bible says, "Cast your burden on the LORD, and He will support you; He will never allow the righteous to be shaken" (Ps. 55:22). Peter wrote, "Cast all your anxiety on him because he cares for you" (1 Pet. 5:7 NIV).

Sometimes when I have no physical item to spread before the Lord, I've written out my prayer, then, kneeling down, I've laid the papers out before the Lord and read them to Him. This is a powerful and effective procedure, recommended to us by God through the example of Hezekiah. Spreading the letter before the Lord, he prayed:

> LORD of Hosts, God of Israel, who is enthroned above the cherubim, You are God—You alone—of all the kingdoms of the earth. You made the heavens and the earth. Listen closely, LORD, and hear; open Your eyes, LORD, and see; hear all the words that Sennacherib has sent to mock the living God. LORD, it is true that the kings of Assyria have devastated all these countries and their lands and have thrown their gods into the fire; for they were not gods but made by human hands—wood and stone. So they have destroyed them. Now, LORD our God, save us from his hand so that all the kingdoms of the earth may know that You are the LORD—You alone. (Isa. 37:16–20)

Since this proved to be one of the most effective prayers ever uttered in Scripture, resulting in the routing of the most powerful army the world had ever seen, we should take a moment to see what we can learn from it.

Notice that Hezekiah didn't focus on his mess but on his Master. He began by reminding himself of the infinite attributes of His God. He began as Jesus did in the Lord's Prayer when He taught us to pray, "Our Father which art in heaven, Hallowed be thy name" (Matt. 6:9b KJV). Hezekiah said, "LORD of Hosts, God of Israel, who is enthroned above the cherubim, You are God—You alone—of all the kingdoms of the earth. You made the heavens and the earth" (v. 16).

It actually took Hezekiah a little while to get around to the disaster itself. Often in a crisis, I plunge into praying about my problem. "Lord, help! Oh, Lord, alas and alack! What are we going to do? Look at this mess! Look at this danger! Can You not see I'm in great pain! Hurry, God!"

But Hezekiah opened his prayer by concentrating on the person and power of God Himself. After all, God already knew about the problem, but He wanted to use the problem to teach Hezekiah more about Himself. It's impossible to pray a prayer of faith unless our prayers are based and centered on the greatness of the One who said, "All authority has been given to me both in heaven and on earth." Don't become so distracted by your crisis that you disregard your Christ.

Then, he carefully stated the problem and asked for help. He prayed earnestly for deliverance. He prayed specifically. He prayed realistically. He prayed intelligently. He prayed clearly. He reminded God of His promises to Judah. And he recorded his request in writing (or at least someone did), for we still have it inscribed on the pages of Scripture.

Hezekiah closed his prayer by asking that God would be glorified, come what may: *"so that all the kingdoms of the earth may know that You are the Lord—You alone."*

The result of this kind of praying? The prophet Isaiah sent this message to Hezekiah: "The Lord, the God of Israel, says: 'Because you prayed to Me about Sennacherib king of Assyria, this is the word the Lord has spoken against him'" (vv. 21b–22a).

Notice those words: *"Because you prayed to Me."*

God unfailingly responds to sincere, earnest, specific prayer offered in the name of Christ and designed for His glory. That kind of prayer changes things. It alters circumstances. Though it may seem to have no immediate results, tremendous forces are unleashed in heaven and on earth that eventually cause all things to work together for good. Promises are claimed. Lives are changed. Circumstances are corrected. Situations are tweaked.

Strength is imparted. Grace is bestowed. History is put right. Answers are given, though they may take awhile to arrive at their intended destination.

In Hezekiah's case, the angels of heaven were mobilized, the heavenly host was dispatched, and one of the most unusual battles in military history took place. The angel of the Lord killed 185,000 Assyrian soldiers, and Sennacherib returned to his capital, tail between legs, and there he was assassinated in the temple of his pagan god by his own sons (Isa. 37:36–38). The world's most powerful military machine stalled in the face of one man on his knees with his problem spread out before the Lord.

* * *

My favorite book on prayer is an old volume titled *The Kneeling Christian*. In the preface, the anonymous author wrote, "It is not too much to say that all real growth in the spiritual life—all victory over temptation, all confidence and peace in the presence of difficulties and dangers, all repose of spirit in times of great disappointment or loss, all habitual communion with God—depends upon the practice of secret prayer."[2]

Having resolved one emergency with prayer, what of Hezekiah's other crisis? "In those days Hezekiah became terminally ill. The prophet Isaiah son of Amoz came and said to him, 'This is what the LORD says: "Put your affairs in order, for you are about to die; you will not recover."' Then Hezekiah turned his face to the wall and prayed to the LORD" (Isa. 38:1–2).

The Lord was again moved by Hezekiah's earnest prayer, and He sent this word: "I have heard your prayer; I have seen your tears. Look, I am going to add 15 years to your life." And God confirmed His answer with an unusual miracle, causing the shadow

---

2. An Unknown Christian, *The Kneeling Christian* (Grand Rapids, MI: Zondervan, n.d.), 5.

running down the staircase to reverse itself by ten steps, signaling that God has the power to do whatever He has promised.

The Bible teaches that prayers of a righteous person are powerful and effective (James 5:16). Hymnist Fanny Crosby said, "All must have their sorrows and disappointments, but we must never forget that Jesus will answer our prayers for our good, and answer them so much more fully and completely than we have dared to dream."[3]

In other words, prayer really works. Now, if you actually believed that, would it make a difference in your daily schedule? In your attitude? In your life?

One of the most encouraging biographies I've ever read is that of Charles Fuller (1887–1968), a Los Angeles native who graduated from Biola University and became the pastor of Calvary Church in Los Angeles.

In the late 1920s and early 1930s, Fuller became involved in buying and selling orange groves in Southern California, and the enterprise was very successful, especially when oil was found on one of the groves.

The Great Depression struck America in October 1929, and by 1931, some of Fuller's financial deals were beginning to go awry. He found himself unable to meet his personal financial obligations, and his fledgling radio broadcast was far from paying for itself. At the same time, his son fell ill to persistent and prolonged attacks of bronchitis. Charles, a noted pastor, faced the humiliation of having his home auctioned from under him to pay his mounting debts. His wife recorded in her journal, "No money to meet bills . . . It is almost more than Charles can bear. He is *so* depressed, *so* burdened that he says he can stand no more."

---

3. Bernard Ruffin, *Fanny Crosby* (Pilgrim Press), 222.

But things grew worse. Their son's health collapsed, and he hovered near the grave. On January 8, 1932, as Charles was at the lawyer's office trying to stave off disaster, his wife called to say that Dannie, age six, was in critical condition and had grown so weak that a pulse was no longer discernible.

Somehow Dannie pulled through, but the stress and strain of their multiple problems so exhausted Charles that when he stood in the pulpit of Calvary Church each Sunday, he wondered whether he could last through the sermon.

So great was their extremity that Charles had to use his wife's inheritance, which her father had carefully set aside and left to her. When it was suddenly gone, she felt embittered and angry.

Then she had to have extensive surgery.

At about the same time, Calvary Church decided it wanted a new pastor, and Charles felt compelled to resign. The morning after his final sermon, the nation's economic depression deepened. President Roosevelt closed all the banks.

Five days later, Long Beach suffered a severe earthquake that killed 115 people and caused millions of dollars of damage. About the same time, one of Charles Fuller's business partners declared bankruptcy, and Charles incurred additional debt.

One morning in August 1933, Mrs. Fuller felt she could bear the stress and strain no longer. When Charles left home to go into Los Angeles and plot his next moves to remain solvent, she went into her study and in desperation started reading one of Charles Haddon Spurgeon's sermons on prayer. He had preached it in London more than seventy years before, and the text was Jeremiah 33:3: "Call unto Me, and I will answer thee, and shew thee great and mighty things, which thou knowest not" (KJV).

She later said, "When I called upon God in desperation in August, 1933, he answered me by directing me *unmistakably* to the library shelf on which this book stood and to *this* sermon.

It brought great comfort and enabled me to trust God and to await the unfolding of His plans for us."

Daniel Fuller later wrote, "She said that God lifted her burden so remarkably that morning that when my father returned exhausted from another day of negotiations in a lawyer's office, she was able to tell him, 'Never mind how black things look now. God has assured me that He has great and mighty things in store for us for the future—things which we can't even imagine now.'"

So it happened. Charles Fuller began preaching on the radio in 1937. He helped pioneer radio evangelism, and his Old-Fashioned Revival Hour on the Mutual Broadcasting System (and later on CBS) was heard live from Long Beach every Saturday night on more than six hundred stations. He became one of the most respected evangelists of his time and later went on to help found Fuller Seminary, which is named in his honor.

In one of his first broadcasts, Dr. Fuller said:

> I pass on to you a little of the comfort wherewith
> Mrs. Fuller and I have been comforted. We have come
> to know God in a new way because of the trials we have
> been going through these past three years. We have
> known what it is to have much sickness; financial losses;
> to have those turn against us and seek to hurt us who we
> thought were true friends; to have our only child brought
> down to death's door on two occasions, and to have
> gone before the microphone, after sleepless nights, so
> burdened and cast down I did not know whether I could
> preach—whether when I opened my mouth the words
> would come. Excuse these personal references, friends,
> I mention them only briefly as a testimony because I
> want to tell you that after going through all this and
> much more, Mrs. Fuller and I know that God is able—

that His promises are true. We never could have known the sweetness of trusting God had we not come to the place where we ourselves could do nothing. We never could have known how precious it is to rest on (God's Word), and having committed all to Him and waiting to see Him work, if we had not been sorely tested.[4]

What a wonderful promise: *"Call to Me and I will show you great and mighty things which you do not know."* That doesn't mean that God is going to do exactly what we wish, as we wish, when we wish, how we wish. His ways are mysterious and marvelous, and He answers in His own way and in His own time; nevertheless, prayer moves His hand, touches His heart, and changes this world, and so our multiple problems have an unfailing way of working for our benefit.

Problems Are Really Opportunities

Hezekiah's story also shows us that problems are really opportunities. Mother Teresa once instructed her associates to refrain from using the word "problem" in her presence. Instead, she told them to say "gift." She understood that every problem is an occasion to seek God's solution and thus to improve our lives and our world a bit at a time.

Occasionally when I've faced a crisis and haven't handled it too well, my wife, Katrina, has taken a different course: "What a great opportunity to trust God!" she tells me. Perhaps that's what she would have told Hezekiah in the face of his mounting difficulties. When Assyrian forces surrounded Jerusalem demanding terms of surrender, the Assyrian field commander issued a threatening challenge. He directly shouted a message to

---

4. Daniel P. Fuller, *The Story of Charles E. Fuller: Give the Winds a Mighty Voice* (Waco, TX: Word, 1972), 87–103.

Hezekiah, asking him, "What are you basing your confidence on? ... Who are you trusting in?" (Isa. 36:4–5).

This Assyrian general unwittingly cut to the very heart of the spiritual purposes of God in allowing problems and perils to threaten His people. These are faith-building episodes for God's people, because the Lord values faith more than nearly anything else in the lives of His children. Without faith it is impossible to please Him.

As I write these words, I've just returned from a meeting with a man I deeply admire—Dr. Ed Dobson. Four years ago, Ed was diagnosed with amyotrophic lateral sclerosis (ALS). Recently he spoke candidly of the deep, dark struggles that tore into his soul and he described his feelings by saying it was like descending into the gloom and doom of the tomb of Lazarus.

But he added, "The book of Hebrews says, 'God has said, "Never will I leave you; never will I forsake you."' So we say with confidence, 'The Lord is my helper; I will not be afraid. What can man do to me?'"

Ed said, "When I would sink into despair I would repeat those words over and over until they began to take hold of me."

I can't fully empathize with his disease, but I do understand Ed's approach. Sometimes in difficulty, I've had to find a promise and concentrate all my mental energies on that promise until it took hold of me and I began to turn my fear into faith.

The psalmist said,

This is my comfort in my affliction:
Your promise has given me life. . . .
Trouble and distress have overtaken me,
but Your commands are my delight.
(Ps. 119:50, 143)

Hezekiah experienced this, too, and not only for himself; he led his entire nation to trust God with fresh faith. In 2 Chronicles 32, we're told that Hezekiah took quick actions to fortify his military positions and strengthen the city's defenses. Then he gathered the population of Jerusalem in the main city square and encouraged the people with one of the most unusual political speeches ever recorded: "Be strong and courageous! Don't be afraid or discouraged before the king of Assyria or before all the multitude with him, for there are more with us than with him. He has only human strength, but we have the LORD our God to help us and to fight our battles" (vv. 7–8a).

And the people gained confidence from Hezekiah's speech. If Judah gained confidence from Hezekiah, where did Hezekiah find it? Perhaps from his spiritual adviser, the prophet Isaiah, who said, "In quietness and confidence shall be your strength" (Isa. 30:15b NKJV).

As I wrote this chapter, I received an e-mail from a young couple, Micah and Becky Derby, who are very dear to me. They're young missionaries on furlough with little boys—toddlers, twins. For a year, they've been driving to church after church, raising their financial support, and they were planning to return to France in only a few months.

Confidence

One of the great biblical synonyms for "faith" is "confidence." Look at the way this term occurs in the book of Psalms:

- Psalm 27:3: "Though an army deploy against me, my heart is not afraid; though war break out against me, still I am confident."
- Psalm 57:7: "My heart is confident. God, my heart is confident. I will sing; I will sing praises."
- Psalm 71:5–6a: "You are my hope, Lord GOD, my confidence from my youth. I have leaned on You from birth."
- Psalm 78:7a: "Put . . . confidence in God."
- Psalm 108:1: "My heart is confident, God; I will sing; I will sing praises with the whole of my being."
- Psalm 112:1a, 7: Happy is the man who fears the LORD. . . . He will not fear bad news; his heart is confident, trusting in the LORD.

Then Becky was suddenly diagnosed with breast cancer. We were worried about her, and the news was discouraging. But here's how she ended her update: "As I write this, I have the radio on and in the background, I hear Chris Tomlin's song 'How Great Is Our God.' With everything that is in me, I believe these words. I don't know why this has happened in our lives, but I do know that it is an opportunity to glorify our Father and that is what we want to do. We want to be a testimony to those we come in contact with that our God is great, that He is good, and that we can trust Him."

Jeremiah 17:7–8a says, "Blessed is the man who trusts in the LORD, whose confidence indeed is the LORD. He will be like a tree planted by water: it sends its roots out toward a stream, it doesn't fear when heat comes, and its foliage remains green."

Hebrews 10:35a says, "So don't throw away your confidence."

In 1 John 5:14 we read, "Now this is the confidence we have before Him: whenever we ask anything according to His will, He hears us."

Confidence is believing in the presence, the power, and the promises of God. Over the past several years, I've begun to realize that God values faith and confidence above almost all else. It was lack of confidence that condemned the ten spies to death. It was lack of faith that sent the children of Israel into forty years of exile in the desert. On the other hand, it was the sturdy faith of Joshua and Caleb that saved their lives and equipped them to lead the new generation of Israelites into Canaan.

It was lack of confidence that made King Saul tremble before the rants and raves of Goliath. It was the unflinching faith of young David that brought the giant to earth and routed the forces of the enemy.

Everywhere Jesus went, He inspected people for their faith. Just thumb through Matthew's Gospel and notice how often Jesus said things like: *Where is your faith? I tell you, I have not found such faith in Israel, According to your faith be it unto you, Why were you afraid, O you of little faith. Woman, you have great faith. O unbelieving generation, how long shall I stay with you? If you have faith as small as a mustard seed . . . nothing shall be impossible for you. I tell you the truth, if you have faith and do not doubt . . . if you believe you will receive whatever you ask for in prayer . . . .*

The Bible says that without faith, it's impossible for us to please God. And the Lord allows trials and troubles to come into our lives to exercise and build up this essential quality of soul confidence, inner composure, and quietness.

Faith is not a blind, frenzied belief that God will do exactly what I'm insisting He do. It isn't asking for things I badly want, then expecting God to grant them regardless of His own wisdom and judgment.

Faith is trusting God even when He doesn't answer our prayers as we'd hoped. It rests in the confidence that His plan for us is best even if, at the time, we can't see how it could be so. As we grow in Christ, we also come to understand that faith is seeking God's will through His Word and prayer, then waiting before Him with sanctified insistence until our needs are granted.

Rev. E. M. Bounds wrote, "Faith and prayer select the things, and God commits Himself to do the very things which faith and persevering prayer nominate and petition for Him to accomplish. . . . Faith gives birth to prayer, and grows stronger, strikes deeper, rises higher, in the struggles and wrestlings of mighty petitioning."

Faith is undaunted when God delays sending the answer or resolving the problem. As Bounds said, "Faith accepts the conditions—knows there will be delays in answering prayer, and regards such delays as times of testing, in the which, it is privilege to show its mettle, and the stern stuff of which it is made."[5]

---

5. E. M. Bounds, *The Complete Works of E. M. Bounds* (Grand Rapids, MI: Baker, 1990), 18, 19.

Faith is the quietness and confidence that God is in control of all the circumstances of my life, even when it appears that chaos reigns and things couldn't be worse. It's resting in Jesus Christ and in His Word, like the old song that says:

Jesus, I am resting, resting,
In the joy of what Thou art;
I am finding out the greatness
Of Thy loving heart.

Geneva Walker, seventy-one, is a friend of mine and the mother of a deacon in my church. She's a cautious driver with a spotless record, no wrecks, tickets, or problems. But on a particular Wednesday last year as she made a left turn on her way to work, another car plowed into the right side of her vehicle.

En route to the hospital, Geneva prayed, asking God to show her why He had allowed this to happen. She didn't believe in accidents. So why, Geneva wondered, had this happened?

Within three hours she had an answer. Though she didn't seem badly injured, doctors in the emergency room ordered a set of X-rays. The technician noticed a disturbing image on the film. There was a tumor on her kidney. Further tests showed it was malignant, and surgery was scheduled. The cancerous kidney was successfully removed, with no further treatments required. Had it not been for her accident, the cancer would not have been detected until too late. "God allowed that accident," Geneva said, "for my good. It literally saved my life."

Faith takes for granted that God has a purpose and that it will, sooner or later, turn out well, sometimes even to the saving of our lives.

Pride Is Really Harmful

The third benefit of anguish is learning that pride is really harmful. Hezekiah was a great man who became king while young and led his nation in restoring the worship of Almighty God. He was a politician but also a preacher. He was royalty, but he was also a revivalist. Yet he wasn't a perfect man. The Bible tells us that a deeply ingrained thread of wickedness wound through his heart. He was afflicted with pride. The writer of 2 Chronicles stated it plainly when he wrote: "Because his heart was proud, Hezekiah didn't respond according to the benefit that had come to him" (32:25).

But look at what Hezekiah prayed after he had been delivered from Assyria and healed of his illness: "I will walk humbly all my years because of this anguish of my soul. . . . Surely it was for my benefit that I suffered such anguish" (Isa. 38:15b, 17a NIV).

God allows trials in our lives because we have a strong core of inner pride and self-sufficiency that works to our long-term detriment. Problems are God's way of showing us we don't have sufficient resources within ourselves to solve every problem or right every wrong. We have to turn to Him, surrender those things into His hands, and let Him have His way. Peter drew a connection between having a humble heart and being able to cast our cares on the Lord when he wrote: "'God resists the proud, but gives grace to the humble.' Humble yourselves therefore . . . casting all your care upon Him, because He cares about you" (1 Pet. 5:5b–7).

Problems dislodge our core of self-sufficient pride, drive us to the Lord, teach us humility, and enable us to trust Him with our cares. In the process we learn that it is for our benefit that we are afflicted.

The Pieces Do Fit Together

Hezekiah survived his thirty-ninth year, and he had fifteen more years during which he could look back over that one terrible year and see how God used it all for good and converted his anguish into alleluias. Turning to Matthew's Gospel, we find Hezekiah in the lineage of the Messiah. He was a link in the chain of promise, and God proved Himself faithful.

In 1939, William Sangster assumed leadership of Westminster Central Hall, a Methodist church near London's Westminster Abbey. During his first worship service he announced to his stunned congregation that Britain and Germany were officially at war. He quickly converted the church basement into an air-raid shelter, and for 1,688 nights Sangster ministered to the various needs of all kinds of people. At the same time, he somehow managed to write, to preach gripping sermons, to earn a Ph.D., and to lead hundreds to Christ. He became known as Wesley's successor in London and was esteemed as the most beloved British preacher of his era.

Sometime after the war, Sangster was diagnosed with progressive muscular atrophy. For three years he slowly died, becoming progressively more paralyzed, finally able to move only two fingers. But his attitude didn't falter, for when first learning of his illness, Sangster made four rules for himself. Many people have rules for living. Sangster composed four rules for dying: "I will never complain. I will keep the home bright. I will count my blessings. I will try to turn it to gain."[6]

He did all those things. And thus the work of God was displayed in his life, and in his death.

God turns all things to gain, works all things to good, and uses all things for our benefit. Even enemy invasions and terminal illnesses.

---

6. From a clipping in my files.

God takes the B,
> the A,
> the D,
And turns them into GOOD.
We don't know how He does this thing,
Or even why He should.
> It always works,
> it never fails
For those whose hearts are true;
All things may be against us,
but Christ makes all things new.

He takes the S,
> the A,
> the D,
And turns them into GLAD,
Though it may take a while to see
How good can come from bad.
> Don't falter, then,
> or faint or fail,
Just search His Word and rest;
Though it may differ from our own
His plan is always best.

CHAPTER 15

All Things Work Out for the Spreading of the Gospel

While driving to Louisville a couple of years ago to see my grandchildren, I felt a sudden pop and puff, and my car lurched to one side. I barely reached the right shoulder of the road, and it wasn't much of a shoulder. I couldn't open my driver's door because of trucks and cars racing over a little hill and a hump on Interstate 65, but to remain in the vehicle was dangerous because it was barely off the road.

With effort, I crawled across the seat and squeezed between the passenger's door and the guardrail, then called the automobile club from a safe distance and waited for help. After a while, a patrol car pulled up, a local sheriff's deputy. I told him I was fine, but he wanted to stay with me until help arrived because it was a dangerous spot. I'd be safer in the car with him, he said, with flashing blue lights. So I spent forty-five minutes in his squad car, waiting for the tow truck to arrive. It was time well spent. We talked about his family, his divorce, his little boy, and about his spiritual needs. Later I sent him a set of the two children's books I'd written, and it became clear to me why God allowed my tire to blow out. What seemed like a dangerous inconvenience turned into an evangelistic opportunity.

When we accept this as a perpetual pattern in the Christian life, it changes the way we look at adversity. British preacher Charles Haddon Spurgeon hit on this when he wrote, "Your sufferings, your losses, and persecutions shall make you a platform, from which the more vigorously and with greater power you shall witness for Christ Jesus."[1]

Something similar happened to me several years ago while vacationing in Gatlinburg, Tennessee. I walked out of our hotel room to find that someone had shattered the window of my car during the night, apparently with a baseball bat or some such device. The hotel refused to assume liability, and I was upset, but there was nothing I could do except to find a glass dealer. Later, a young man named Jim came with his truck to repair the damage. I was fuming, but I managed to watch with admiration as Jim systematically disassembled the van's door, removed the splinters of glass, and slipped a new window into place. His young assistant resembled him, and I asked if they were related.

"He's my little brother," said Jim. "He's filling in till I can find someone to replace my coworker who died last week. He had a wife and two kids. Just forty-two. Died of a heart attack."

As it turned out, that gave me an opening to gently and carefully share a word of gospel witness with Jim, to talk with him about the brevity and the uncertainty of life, and to speak with him about our need for a Savior. I realized that an apparent random act of destruction was actually a divine appointment for the sharing of the gospel.

---

1. Charles H. Spurgeon, *Morning and Evening*.

Over and over, if we train ourselves to see it, our worst problems become our best pulpits. All these things become arenas for sharing our faith with others.

All Things

- Romans 8:28 tells us that all things work together for our good.
- Ephesians 1:11 tells us that all things work together in conformity with the purpose of God's will.
- Genesis 50:20 tells us that all things work together for the good of others.
- Philippians 1:12 tells us that all things work together for the advancing of the gospel.

In writing to friends in the city of Philippi, Paul said, "Now I want you to know, brothers, that what has happened to me has actually resulted in the advancement of the gospel" (Phil. 1:12).

Notice the phrase "what has happened to me." Alexander Maclaren said, "That is Paul's minimizing euphemism for the grim realities of imprisonment."[2]

The apostle Paul had been planning a fourth missionary trip that would take him into western Europe. In only ten remarkable years, he had effectively evangelized the major cities of eastern Europe and western Asia. Along with his associates, he had planted churches in virtually all the major cities between Antioch and Athens. Now he had wanted to press the gospel westward, past Italy, beyond Rome, and on toward Spain, Gaul, and Britain. But at that moment, he was seized in Jerusalem, imprisoned in Caesarea, and placed under house arrest in Rome.

Now he was sitting in chains while his dreams of evangelizing Europe were fading away. Time was passing him by. His health wasn't good, and there was no quick end to his legal problems. Furthermore, it was terrifying to be a political prisoner in the

---

2. Alexander Maclaren, *Expositions of the Holy Scriptures: Second Corinthians VII to End, Galatians, and Philippians* (Grand Rapids, MI: Baker, 1982), 212.

ironlike vice of the ancient empire of Rome, to be at the mercy of an emperor, and to be locked up by the most brutal soldiers the world had thus far produced.

Paul's simple phrase summarizing all this was: "what has happened to me."

I think he put it that way for two reasons. First, he didn't feel like going into details. He wasn't one to share every facet of his problems with others.

But there was another reason Paul spoke generally. It was for the same reason he referred to his illness as "a thorn in the flesh" in 2 Corinthians 12. Paul never told us what his thorn was, and for two thousand years Christian scholars have been curious as to the nature of Paul's malady. Why didn't he tell us? In Philippians 1, why didn't he describe the specific things that had happened to him? I believe Paul sometimes dealt in personal generalities that we might more easily apply his lessons to our lives.

Few of us will ever contract the exact disease that afflicted Paul, but all of us will face sickness and disease. Few of us will ever be thrown into a Roman prison, but all of us will have negative things happen. This universal phrase—"what has happened to me"—is a euphemism for the disasters, tragedies, difficulties, and troubles of life.

What things have happened to you? You didn't cause them, at least not knowingly or deliberately. You didn't want them. You didn't ask for them. They simply happened. They came uninvited and unwelcomed like a bunch of thugs that showed up at the party, elbowed their way in, and were loathe to leave. All of us can identify with these little words: "what has happened to me."

Suddenly, our whole perception changes when we read the entire sentence: "Now I want you to know, brothers, that what has happened to me has really served to advance the gospel" (NIV).

This word translated "advance" is a Greek word—*prokope*—used in Bible times for pioneers cutting their way through forests, pressing onward, and opening new frontiers. It was used of an army advancing over land and across mountains and barreling forward to conquer new territory. The word *gospel* means the Good News that God became a man named Jesus Christ who died and rose again to reconcile the human race to Himself and to give us everlasting life through the forgiveness gained by the shedding of His blood.

Paul was saying, "My shattered dreams, my demolished plans, my hopes for taking the gospel to western Europe, my incarceration, my Roman prison, my chains and confinement—all of this has fallen out rather for the furtherance of the gospel."

So here's the principle: God not only works all things for our good and for the good of others, He not only resolves all things according to the council of His will, He also causes all things to work out for the furtherance of the gospel. He takes the circumstances of life and makes the platforms and arenas in which the gospel can be shared. He takes our bad news and turns it into opportunities for sharing His Good News.

Think of a negative situation in your life. Ask the Lord how He intends to make it a platform for the gospel. Is your trial a testimony in disguise? Can it open a door for your message?

People in Our Pathway

In this text in Philippians 1, Paul demonstrated three ways God turned his problems into opportunities for evangelism. First, problems have a way of putting into our pathways certain people we'd otherwise not meet. As a result of his problems, Paul found a whole new audience for his message. His circumstances actually aided his great purpose of evangelizing the lost. Verses 12–13 say: "I want you to know, brothers, that what has happened to me has actually resulted in the advancement of the gospel, so that it has become known throughout the whole imperial guard, and to everyone else, that my imprisonment is for Christ."

Because of his incarceration, Paul had gained access into two groups that were very difficult to reach with the gospel. In fact, these two groups were, humanly speaking, off limits to any kind of evangelistic effort.

The first group was the Praetorian Guard. These were the imperial troops, an army within the army, consisting of nine thousand elite soldiers who personally served the Roman emperor. It had been instituted by Caesar Augustus. Because he was a high-profile political prisoner, Paul was entrusted to the Praetorian Guard, and he was apparently chained, wrist to wrist, with an endlessly rotating number of these soldiers, probably several a day, in shifts.

Can you imagine being chained to the apostle Paul for hours at a time? As these men got to know him as he shared his testimony, wrote his letters, counseled those who came to him, prayed with his friends, and preached to small groups, one soldier after another came to faith in Christ. The gospel was spreading among the top echelons of the Roman army. As troops were mobilized to far-flung corners of the empire, these soldiers became missionaries in disguise, taking the gospel to places where Paul himself would never journey.

Another group was also being saved. Paul simply says in verse 13, "it has become known throughout the whole imperial guard, and to everyone else."

Everyone else was a term that certainly included (but was not limited to) members of the royal household. At the end of Philippians, Paul wrote, "All the saints greet you, but especially those from Caesar's household" (4:22).

So the great lesson of Philippians 1:12–13 is that God has His purposes for our lives when our dreams are shattered, when our plans are changed, and when trouble and limitations come into our lives. He intends His children to consider these times as special opportunities to evangelize.

Isobel Kuhn was a missionary to China who became a well-known writer of Christian classics. Ruth Bell Graham once recommended her books to me, and I've been reading them ever since. Isobel's last book, written as she was dying of cancer, is titled *In the Arena.* I've thumbed through my paperback copy so many times the pages are coming out and I have to secure it with a rubber band.

In this book, Isobel looked back over her life and described various obstacles, difficulties, and heartbreaks she had encountered. By the grace of God, she said, she had come to realize that all of them had become platforms and arenas in which God could be glorified and His Word spread to those who needed it.

This little book has twelve chapters, each of which describes a set of circumstances in Isobel's life that resulted in the advancement of the gospel. The chapter titles are:

1. Obstacles
2. Uncongenial Work
3. Secret Choices
4. Crossed Nature
5. Frustrations
6. Extinguished Candle-flames
7. Small Harassments
8. Taut Nerves
9. Seeming Defeat
10. Between the Scissors' Knives
11. Stranded at the World's End
12. Dread Disease

Every trial and tribulation became a testimony, and that's the universal lesson for all God's heroes. The great Dutch Christian and Holocaust survivor Corrie ten Boom once wrote an article titled "My Unforgettable Christmas." It was Christmas of 1944, and she was in the hospital barracks of Ravensbruck, the Nazi prison camp. There were Christmas trees here and there in the streets between the barracks, but underneath them were the bodies of dead prisoners who had been thrown out. Corrie had tried to talk to some of her fellow sufferers about Christmas, but they were in no mood for it, and finally she had decided to keep quiet.

In the middle of the night, she heard a child calling out, "Mommy! Come to Oelie. Oelie feels so alone." Corrie went and found the child, who turned out not young after all but instead feeble-minded. Oelie was emaciated, and a bandage of toilet paper covered an incision from surgery on her back. Through that long, dark night, Corrie stayed with Oelie and told her about Jesus, how He came to earth as a baby at Christmas, how He loved us, how He died for our sins, how He had risen from death, and how He was now in heaven preparing a beautiful house for us. Oelie learned to trust Christ as her Savior, how to pray to Him, and how to gain strength from Him. And in writing the story years later, Corrie ten Boom added these words: "Then I knew why I had to spend this Christmas in Ravensbruck."[3]

Somehow in the wonder-working providence of God, our worst problems become our best pulpits. I've never forgotten about something that happened to my friend Evelyn Hersey, missionary to Japan who is now in heaven. For years she had sought to win a certain man to Christ. She eventually developed cancer and returned to America for medical treatments. As she was dying, she called her Japanese friend and said, "Don't worry about

---

3. Corrie ten Boom, "My Unforgettable Christmas," *Moody Monthly,* December 1976, 27.

me, for I'm bound for heaven. I just want you to know that we love you and I'll be praying for you." The man shortly afterward became a Christian. He said, "How could I fail to trust a Savior who gave my friend the kindness and love to pray for me even when she was sick and dying?"

Another friend and former church member Celecca Cutts once told me of a time when she was sitting in a church service and the minister asked, "Will those of you who are willing to do anything necessary to lead others to Christ please raise your hands?" Celecca cautiously lifted her hand.

While returning from nursing school a few days later, Celecca saw another driver coming toward her, trying to pass an eighteen-wheeler. She swerved. Her car slammed into the truck and rolled over three times before careening down an embankment.

For days, Celecca hovered between coma and consciousness. Her mother sat by her bed, holding her hand and praying. In the same semiprivate room, another mother sat by her diseased daughter, listening. By the time Celecca recovered, her mother had won both the other mother and her daughter to the Lord.

God turns tragedies into testimonies and uses emergencies for evangelism.

If that's true, what do we need to do? There are four important ingredients that we've got to throw into the bowl.

1. Memorize a verse or series of verses that will enable you to share Christ with someone. Learn a simple plan of salvation. It can be as short as Romans 6:23: "For the wages of sin is death, but the gift of God is eternal life in Christ Jesus our Lord." Many a person has been saved by the sound of this one simple verse.
2. Train yourself to look at life's situations as opportunities to witness. One of the first things to ask yourself in a

moment of difficulty is, "Is there someone here God wants me to reach?" It makes a huge difference in your attitude.

3. Go ahead and open your mouth. If you get half a chance, say a word for the Lord. The Bible says, "Let the redeemed of the Lord say so."

4. Don't underestimate how God can eventually use even a simple witness. Our labor in the Lord is not in vain, and His Word does not return to Him void.

* * *

In the summer of 1976, the Christian organization Campus Crusade for Christ sponsored a retreat for the wives of staff members. It was in northern Colorado, near Estes Park. By mid-afternoon, it had begun to rain, and at 7:35 p.m., the National Weather Service issued a severe thunderstorm warning. Suddenly, the bottom fell out of the sky, and more than eleven inches of rain fell in only four hours. The narrow canyon where the women were meeting was filled with a deluge of water twenty feet high. One hundred thirty-nine people died in the Big Thompson flood, including seven of the Campus Crusade staff wives.

Several weeks later, as the Campus Crusade family mourned for those they had lost, someone hit on a unique and novel idea to honor them. It was decided to make their last moments on earth a tribute to the faithfulness of God. With the full approval of their families, Campus Crusade placed ads in major newspapers across America. The advertisement said: "These seven women lost their lives in the Colorado flood, but they are still alive and they have a message for you."

Those advertisements reached approximately 150 million people around the world, and thousands of people wrote back to say they had received Jesus Christ as Savior as a result of the tragic loss of those seven women. The American ambassador to an overseas country got in touch to say that his life had been changed by the words he read, and he later helped open that foreign nation to the work of Campus Crusade.

The Big Thompson Flood was widely reported in 1976 and has been written about many times since. To this day, Christian leaders marvel how the Lord used this tragedy as a platform for evangelism, and how a sadness of lives lost became the glory of lives transformed forever through the power of Jesus Christ.[4]

We see things like this over and over in the two-thousand-year sweep of Christianity. Nothing creates revival or spreads the gospel like those negative events orchestrated by the Devil but coopted and used by the Lord. Suffering puts a new set of people in our pathway.

Courage in Our People

According to Philippians 1, there's a second way in which negative life events serve to advance the gospel. It puts courage in those watching us. It puts stamina in other Christians who observe it. It motivates them to share Christ themselves and to do so more courageously and fearlessly.

Paul wrote, "Now I want you to know, brothers, that what has happened to me has actually resulted in the advancement of the gospel, so that it has become known throughout the whole imperial guard, and to everyone else, that my imprisonment is for Christ. Most of the brothers in the Lord have gained confidence from my imprisonment and dare even more to speak the message fearlessly" (vv. 12–14).

Notice the words he used. Not all, but *most* of the brothers in the Lord were encouraged to speak the word of God, and with renewed boldness. The Amplified Bible renders verse 14: "And

---

4. This story is summarized from eyewitness and newspaper accounts and from information gleaned from materials produced by Bill Bright and Campus Crusade for Christ.

[also] most of the brethren have derived fresh confidence in the Lord because of my chains and are much more bold to speak and publish fearlessly the Word of God [acting with more freedom and indifference to the consequences]."

I don't know if this is true for you, but often I find that nothing motivates me like the example of someone else. When I first began sharing my faith with others, it was a college friend who spurred me on by his example. We're all impressionable people, and we "catch" courage and boldness from the examples of others.

Many years ago in Scotland, the nefarious churchman Cardinal David Beaton began persecuting Lutheran and Protestant preachers and condemning evangelical Christians to the stake. One of those who died was Patrick Hamilton.

Cardinal Beaton didn't realize he was making heroes, martyrs, and saints from ordinary, everyday Christians. He was providing these heroic men and women a powerful platform for their testimony. One man finally went to the cardinal and told him he was ruining his own cause. "If you burn any more you should burn them in low cellars," advised the man, "for the smoke of Mr. Patrick Hamilton has infected as many as it blew upon."[5]

It reminds me of a story about John Wycliffe. He was called the "Morning Star of the Reformation" because he started preaching the pure gospel in the midst of corrupt days. He would have been burned at the stake himself had he not died first of natural causes. He was buried in the churchyard, but forty-one years later, still hated by his enemies, his bones were exhumed, burned, and thrown into a nearby brook known as the Swift River.

A biographer wrote, "They burnt his bones to ashes and cast

---

5. Alexander Maclaren, *Expositions of the Holy Scriptures: Second Corinthians VII to End, Galatians, and Philippians* (Grand Rapids, MI: Baker, 1982), 215. In the original quotation the word "reek" is used. Maclaren put the word "smoke" in parentheses to update the term for his readers.

them into the Swift, a neighboring brook running hard by. Thus the brook conveyed his ashes into the Avon, the Avon into the Severn, the Severn into the narrow seas and they into the main ocean. And so the ashes of Wycliffe are symbolic of his doctrine, which is now spread throughout the world."

Whenever we stand for Christ at a difficult time, it not only evangelizes the lost, it motivates the saved. In the Philippians text, Paul went on to say that not everyone who started sharing Christ did so from the purest of motives. Some were motivated by envy and jealousy. Clergy are not immune to envy and jealousy, as I know from personal experience and from looking into my own heart. I can imagine some of the first-century evangelists thinking to themselves, "As long as Paul was in circulation, he was the greatest preacher and everyone talked about him. With him out of the way, our ministry will seem more prominent."

Paul's attitude about it was: Praise the Lord anyway!

"What does it matter?" he wrote. "Just that in every way, whether out of false motives or true, Christ is proclaimed. And in this I rejoice. Yes, and I will rejoice" (v. 18).

That's a great question to store away for future use: What does it matter?

We have little disagreements, or we get our feelings hurt. We notice someone doing something from an inferior motivation; we see something that makes us want to react. We hear an opinion contrary to our own, we don't get our way, or we spot a bit of hypocrisy.

Maybe we should simply say: What does it matter?

Blessed are people who know how to shrug, smile, and go on. Blessed are people with ducks' backs.

"What does it matter?" wrote Paul. The important thing was that in every way, whether from false motives or true, Christ was preached. And because of that he rejoiced.

Trials and troubles bring people into our pathways. They allow us to be a motivating example to others. And there is a third thing here, a third way in which the imprisonment of the apostle Paul served to advance the gospel. It isn't *in* the text; it *is* the text.

Ink in our Pens

Paul's imprisonment put ink in his pen and created the occasion in which he authored his famous Prison Epistles, including Philippians, Ephesians, and Colossians. The Devil thought he was shutting Paul up, and instead he created a situation in which Paul ministered to the ages. Who can ever calculate how many millions have come to Christ through sermons based in the Prison Epistles? Had it not been for this disruption, this disaster, we would never have had some of our greatest passages of Scripture.

We would not have the passage in Philippians 2 that says: "Let this mind be in you which was also in Christ Jesus, who, being in the form of God, did not consider it robbery to be equal with God, but made Himself of no reputation, taking the form of a bondservant, and coming in the likeness of men. And being found in appearance as a man, He humbled Himself and became obedient to the point of death, even the death of the cross. Therefore God also has highly exalted Him and given Him the name which is above every name, that at the name of Jesus every knee should bow, of those in heaven, and of those on earth, and of those under the earth, and that every tongue should confess that Jesus Christ is Lord, to the glory of God the Father" (vv. 5–11 NKJV).

We would not have the passage in Philippians 3 that says: "Brethren, I do not count myself to have apprehended; but one thing I do, forgetting those things which are behind and reaching forward to those things which are ahead, I press toward the goal for the prize of the upward call of God in Christ Jesus" (vv. 13–14 NKJV).

We would not have the passage in Philippians 4 that says: "Rejoice in the Lord always. Again I will say, rejoice! Let your gentleness be known to all men. The Lord is at hand. Be anxious for nothing, but in everything by prayer and supplication, with thanksgiving, let your requests be made known to God; and the peace of God, which surpasses all understanding, will guard your hearts and minds through Christ Jesus" (vv. 4–7 NKJV).

And we would not have equally precious verses in those other letters Paul wrote from his prison cell.

It's like John Bunyan. The Bedford officials were cruel to him, tearing him away from his family and his little blind daughter, because he wanted to preach as a Baptist minister. He nearly rotted in Bedford Jail for his faith in Christ. He was there for years. But out of his imprisonment came more than sixty books, including the immortal classic *Pilgrim's Progress,* which has helped take Christianity to the ends of the earth and into many a heart.

In my research into the history of hymnology, I discovered— this did not really surprise me—that many of our greatest hymns were written by men and women who faced a period of suffering in life. A good example is Luther Bridges's great gospel song "He Keeps Me Singing." Bridges was an old-time evangelist whose wife and three children perished in a fire. When he received news of their deaths, he nearly lost his mind, but eventually he found strength in the Word of God and from that experience he wrote:

> There's within my heart a melody, Jesus whispers
> > sweet and low:
> "Fear not, I am with thee; peace be still, in all of life's
> > ebb and flow."
> Jesus, Jesus, Jesus, sweetest name I know,
> Fills my every longing, keeps me singing as I go.
> > —Luther Bridges (1910)

I encourage you to keep a journal, write letters, write poems, express your testimony in pen and ink, or send e-mails. Find every way you can to share your testimony of God's faithfulness and to tell others how He keeps you singing.

Our testimonies are forged and crafted in the trials of life, our pain has an evangelistic purpose, our problems become His pulpits, and the things that happen to us turn out for the furtherance of the gospel.

CHAPTER 16

All Things Work Out in Multiple Distresses

One freezing February day in the 1800s, crowds of people gathered on a snow-covered field twelve miles west of Dublin, Ireland. Two men had been feuding, and their dispute had become the talk of the town. Now they had determined to settle the matter by staging a duel. By nightfall, one of the men was dead. His name was John D'Esterre, and the winner of the duel was a famous Irish politician named Daniel O'Connell.

John D'Esterre left behind a young wife named Jane. Only eighteen years old, she already had two small children to support. There was little money in the bank, and immediately after the death of her husband, the bailiffs arrived at her home to seize and appropriate all her husband's goods. When they left, they told her they were also going to confiscate her husband's corpse and sell it to the hospital mortuary to pay some of the remaining debts.

With the help of friends, Jane sneaked her husband's body out of the city that night and hastily buried him in an unmarked grave by lantern light.

Knowing her creditors would never leave her in peace, she decided to flee to Scotland, and there she settled in the little village of Ecclefechan where she sank into a deep depression. One day she took a novel to the river to read for a while, but her heart wasn't in reading. She was too distracted and distraught. Sitting there, her self-pity deepened to dangerous levels, and she contemplated suicide.

Suddenly, Jane heard a noise coming from the other side of the river. It was a young ploughman who had entered his field and was commencing his work. As he wielded the plow behind the animals, he began whistling Christian hymns. The young farmer was well known in the area for being a hymn-whistler. Jane watched him, and something about his spirit and attitude touched her.

She had two small children dependent on her. She was healthy and had her whole life in front of her. If a simple ploughman could display such cheer and enthusiasm for the mundane work of his life, why should not she?

Armed with a new perspective, she returned to Dublin where, shortly afterward, she attended a service at St. George's Church and heard a sermon from John 3:16. Soon she trusted Jesus Christ as her Savior. Jane grew in faith, and God gave her an unusual burden. She began to pray earnestly for her children and for the next twelve generations who would follow her.

One day the Lord brought a new man into Jane's life, a very wealthy man named Captain John Guinness, and the two were married. Jane continued raising her children and praying for her twelve subsequent generations. She asked God to provide a continuing Christian witness in the world through her descendants.

The result? Her son, Grattan, gave away his fortune and became a minister. He preached to thousands and helped trigger the 1859 revival in Ireland in which as many as one hundred thousand people came to Christ in one year. The largest buildings in Ireland could not hold the crowds coming to hear him preach.

From his descendants alone (not to mention the other extending branches of the family tree) has come a host of Christian workers who have traveled the earth with the Good News of Jesus Christ. Even today, the name of Dr. Os Guinness is known around the world. Born to missionary parents in China, he has been a statesman for Christ in his generation.[1]

As I read the remarkable story of Jane Guinness, I marveled at the way God took a series of tragedies and turned them into tools for guiding His children, using their lives, blessing His work, and expanding His kingdom. He took gloomy, hopeless circumstances and used them as a means of bringing the Good News of Christ to hundreds of thousands of people for more than twelve generations in history.

But why do we have to go through the suffering, anxious nights, and hurtful times of life? Could God not accomplish His purposes painlessly?

I've been studying that subject in the ancient book of Job. In many ways, Job is a mysterious book in the Bible—we don't know who wrote it or when—yet in other ways, it clears up a lot of mysteries. Job is the Bible's premier book devoted to the subject of theodicy, which is that branch of theology dealing with the mystery of evil in the universe. If God is so great and so good, why do bad things happen so often to so many people, including each of us? The book of Job presents a very interesting analysis of that question. You can read through the entire book of Job in forty-seven and one half minutes—at least, that's how long it took me. But if you want to put that off till later, I'll tell you the story in briefer form.

Job was a wealthy Middle Eastern sheikh who knew and loved God. As a highly respected member of his city council, he bent

---

1. This story is told in greater detail in a booklet I highly recommend: Derick Bingham, *A Guinness with a Difference: The Story of the Whistling Ploughboy of Ecclefechan* (TBF Thompson Ministries, Londonderry, North Ireland, n.d.).

over backward to help people with their problems. He was kind, fair, generous, and wise. As a husband, he was faithful and had made a covenant with his eyes not to lust after other women. As a father, he was burdened for his children and prayed for them earnestly.

Suddenly, one day Job was hit by multiple disasters. His crops were ruined, his herds stolen, his wealth plundered, and, worst of all, his children killed. Shortly afterward, he developed an awful disease in which his skin erupted in boils that itched and festered, and his body began decaying as though he were already dead.

At first, Job wanted to die, cursing the day of his birth and openly questioning why God didn't kill him and end his suffering. The grave seemed far better to him than his emotional and physical pain. Job had a lot of questions, many of them addressed to God. In fact, as I read through the entire book of Job, I found 290 questions, many of them starting with "Why?"

His friends came to comfort him, and most of the book is a record of their dialogue. Over and over, they told Job that his suffering was caused by unconfessed sin in his life. "If you repent," they said, "God will relieve your distress and resolve your problems." This didn't make any sense to Job for two reasons. First, Job wasn't aware of having committed any supersin that would incur this kind of wrath. Though he didn't claim to be sinless, he did feel he had been relatively moral, ethical, and righteous in his ways. Second, Job noticed that a lot of scoundrels enjoyed a prosperous life, and though they seemed far more sinful than he, these people were living in the lap of luxury.

It's only natural to have questions. Last year, a friend loaned me his spare room at a retreat center in France, and I tried to recover from a bad case of fatigue. Several things had happened to me that I didn't understand. For several years, I had prayed earnestly about a number of issues in my life, things I cared about deeply. I felt in my heart that I knew God's will on these matters. Yet instead of my prayers being answered, the exact opposite had happened.

I was frankly upset with the Lord, and as I paced back and forth in my room, I told Him so. I didn't understand how things so important to me could have gone so badly, especially after I had earnestly given them to Him, praying about them for many years. I still don't have the answers to some of these things, and my faith and confidence have taken some hits. But it's somehow comforting to me that Job had some of the same questions, and his distresses were far greater than mine. He ranted and raved. He wept and wailed. He frustrated his friends and rejected their counsel. He longed for death and wished he'd never been born. He cursed his pain and longed to have it out, face to face, with the Almighty.

But Job never lost his faith in the truth of Romans 8:28. Though that verse hadn't yet been written, the truth of it was extant, and Job worded his own version of it when he told his friends: "Just wait, this is going to work out for the best" (Job 13:16 MSG).

Later, in the New Testament, James suggested that Job is a model for all of us during times of trouble and trial. "Brothers," he said in James 5:10–11, "take the prophets who spoke in the Lord's name as an example of suffering and patience. See, we count as blessed those who have endured. You have heard of Job's endurance and have seen the outcome from the Lord: the Lord is very compassionate and merciful."

Look at Job, said James. When you have problems in your life, study his reactions. Emulate him. Yes, he was hurt and he ranted, raved, and questioned. But he persevered, he trusted God, and he discovered in the end that the Lord is very compassionate and merciful. Rather than being cursed, Job was blessed.

The other day as I sat down and read through this book again, I was struck with Job's three great declarations of faith. Despite his suffering and inner struggles, and in spite of all his questions and pain, he still managed by sheer faith to make three ringing declarations of trust in the Lord, in chapters 13, 19, and 23.

1. "Though He slay me, yet will I trust Him" (Job 13:15a NKJV).
2. "For I know that my Redeemer lives, and He shall stand at last on the earth; and after my skin is destroyed, this I know, that in my flesh I shall see God" (Job 19:25–26 NKJV).
3. "Yet He knows the way I have taken; when He has tested me, I will emerge as pure gold. My feet have followed in His tracks; I have kept to His way and not turned aside. I have not departed from the commands of His lips; I have treasured the words of His mouth more than my daily food" (Job 23:10–12).

At the end of the book, after Job and his friends had exhausted their deliberations, the Lord Himself suddenly appeared in a whirlwind and spoke to Job. God had a few questions of His own. He didn't provide explanations; He asked, in effect, "Job, where were you when I formed the heavens and the earth? Did you teach the eagle to fly? Did you create the great animals and the tiny drops of dew? Don't you think I know what I'm doing? Don't you think I'm big enough to care for My children? Have you forgotten that I work all things for good?"

He was saying, in effect, "Even when you don't understand, I'm the One you should trust." The Lord Jesus Christ summarized the lesson of Job when He told us in John 16:33b: "You will have suffering in this world. Be courageous! I have conquered the world." We walk by faith and not by sight, and without faith it is impossible to please God. Those who serve Him must believe He is able to turn curses into blessings.

In the end, everything did work out for Job, as it will for all God-lovers. Amid his multiple miseries, Job didn't abandon his faith, and he emerged from the valley of pain stronger and happier than ever, capable of ministering hope to people even now, thousands of years later.

Recently, I was discussing this with a friend from college days, Dave Tosi, who pastors a church in West Virginia. He told me that his wife, Marilyn, has been a diabetic since she was twenty-one years old, and her condition has occasionally caused serious health complications. Late in 2002, Marilyn became very sick and was in and out of the hospital. Then her kidneys failed, and she was on dialysis many months.

Just then, a difficult situation arose in the church they were pastoring at the time, and suddenly Dave and Marilyn were out of a job. They couldn't understand it because it was the first time they'd been churchless since God had called them into the ministry. They weren't sure how they were going to make it. It was one blow after another.

One by one, however, their needs were met in unexpected ways. One of the members of their former church sent them a large check every month for their health insurance. Other friends sent money and food. Dave was able to pay off his car loan, so that bill was taken care of. Another friend, an attorney, loaned them his vacation condominium to live in, and it was in an area with an excellent kidney transplant hospital. The greatest gift of all was Marilyn's younger sister donating her kidney.

"Now we look back and see that God allowed me to have that time away from my ministry so that I could take care of Marilyn," Dave told me. "She was able to do almost nothing for months, and I had the joy of caring for her and managing our household without the burdens of a pastorate. As soon as Marilyn recovered, God led us to a wonderful church and we resumed our ministry. It's remarkable, looking back on it, how all our troubles turned out well."

Job would agree.

If we could summarize the primary message of the book of Job, it's this: Life is full of problems and pain; questions are all right, and so is occasional ranting and raving, but don't grow bitter and never throw away your faith. All these things will work for good, and God will turn it to gain as we keep our eyes locked on Him and walk by faith, not by sight.

> Is not Thy grace as mighty now
> As when Elijah felt its power;
> When glory beamed from Moses' brow,
> Or Job endured the trying hour?
>
> Remember, Lord, the ancient days;
> Renew Thy work; Thy grace restore;
> Warm our cold hearts to prayer and praise,
> And teach us how to love Thee more.
>   —William H. Bathurst (1831)

"This sickness will not end in death but is for the glory of God."
—John 11:4a

CHAPTER 17

All Things Work Out in the Cemetery

R ecently, as I sat down for some final editing of this manuscript, my cell phone rang. A friend I had known since college days was sending word to me through his son-in-law. Could I come at once? His wife had just died.

I arrived at the hospital as he was shuffling, stunned and disheveled, from the emergency room. It had happened so suddenly, so unexpectedly. They were enjoying their retirement years, both seemingly in good health. Darrell, who was fascinated by the dramatic arts, was only days away from a starring role in a production sponsored by his church. But that morning as they rose from bed, Sarah had gulped for a breath that didn't come, and Darrell had called 911, then tried to perform CPR. He sobbed on my shoulder, and all I knew to whisper in his ear were the words, "I'm so sorry . . . so sorry."

Going to the hospital chapel, we sat down and immediately started talking about heaven, the mansions prepared for us, the hope within us, how it's far better to be absent from the body but present with the Lord, how happy Sarah was now, and how all things work out for good.

Those are not mere words, but neither are they magical words. They don't instantly banish the tears, but they do stabilize the soul. In some ways, I think of John 11:4 as our Lord's version of Romans 8:28: "This sickness will not end in death but is for the glory of God."

Jesus spoke those words when word came that His friend Lazarus was ill. Jesus tarried where He was, and Lazarus died. But the story doesn't end there. The moment Lazarus died, Christ set out for Bethany where He performed a dramatic miracle, the raising of Lazarus from death to life.

More space is given to the resurrection of Lazarus than to any other miracle in the Gospels, so it's evidently a very important episode in the life of Christ. It comes near the end of Christ's earthly ministry and triggers the chain of events that results in His arrest and crucifixion. But more than anything else, it displays the authority of Jesus Christ over the very processes of death itself and shows us how He can reverse even that, making it work for our good.

Modern visitors to Jerusalem often visit a suburb that lies less than two miles from the Old City and the Temple Mount. There at Bethany, we can still find the traditional site of the tomb of Lazarus. The traditions associated with this tomb stretch back into the earliest centuries of Christian history. Writing in the early 300s, the historian Eusebius said of Bethany, "There the place of Lazarus is still shown," referring to his tomb. In AD 333, a guide pointed out to the Pilgrim of Bordeaux the tomb where Lazarus had been laid. In AD 390, St. Jerome mentions a church built near the place (or tomb) of Lazarus. I've visited that tomb more than once, and though its current appearance and surroundings look different than in biblical times, it makes for meaningful contemplation.

We can all pay this graveyard a visit every time we read John 11, and there we can learn several lessons.

Death Is a Reality

In verse 14b, Jesus bluntly told the disciples: "Lazarus has died." No bones about it. He was dead. Deceased. Departed. His heart stopped beating, his lungs heaved a final time, and suddenly his life processes ceased and death occurred.

His sisters, Mary and Martha, were in the grip of grief, for their beloved brother had not survived his illness. Hearing the news, the disciples were heavyhearted, and Jesus Himself was grieved.

The other day as we drove through the cemetery for a funeral, I remarked to my wife, "Today it seems like only one person in the world has died, and it's a great individual tragedy because it's our friend. But really, thousands of people have died today around the world." In my mind's eye, I pictured the thousands of deathbed scenes and funerals occurring all over the earth at that very moment. It's overwhelming to think about. Demographers tell us that approximately 108 people on this planet die every minute. That's reality.

Recently, as I purchased cemetery plots for my wife and me in East Tennessee, the sales agent took me to several different places in the graveyard to see which ones I wanted to buy. It was a strange experience, looking down at a little plot of ground and knowing that within a short time I'll be buried beneath that plot of grass to wait until Jesus comes. The Bible doesn't deny the reality of death; it explains it, but it doesn't deny it. Lazarus was dead.

Death Is a Phase, Not a Finality

But the story of Lazarus teaches something far greater: Death is a phase, not a finality. For the follower of Jesus Christ, death is a tunnel but not a cave. It's a one-way route to glory, not a dead-end street to oblivion. Jesus used two different phrases in this story to communicate this to us.

First, when He heard that Lazarus was sick, he said, "This sickness will not end in death but is for the glory of God" (v. 4a).

That's the motto we can print in calligraphy and post on the hospital wall of every Christian who ever faces a terminal illness. I could go into the sickbed of any Christian and quote that verse. I don't want to sound cavalier, but after all, these are the words of Jesus. He spoke those words of his friend Lazarus and within ninety-six hours, Lazarus was dead. His sickness included death, but it did not end in death. Death is a phase, not a finality. It's temporary, not terminal.

The second phrase is found later when Jesus said, "Our friend Lazarus has fallen asleep, but I'm on my way to wake him up" (v. 11b). Dying is falling asleep in Jesus. This is New Testament language. This is Jesus-talk.

All three Synoptic Gospels tell us about a ruler named Jairus who sought out Jesus in great urgency, begging Him to come and touch his twelve-year-old daughter who was dying, but before Jesus arrived, the little girl passed away. "They came to the leader's house, and He saw a commotion—people weeping and wailing loudly. He went in and said to them, 'Why are you making a commotion and weeping? The child is not dead but asleep.' They started laughing at Him" (Mark 5:38–40a).

Jesus unceremoniously threw them out, then He took the child's parents and a handful of His disciples and knelt beside the child. Taking the girl's hand, He said a few words to her, and she immediately opened her eyes, looked at them in amazement, rolled off her bed, and started walking around.

She was "not dead but asleep," Jesus had said. "Lazarus is asleep," He explained. That's the way He looked at it.

In Acts 7, we have the account of the first Christian martyred for his faith—Stephen, who was stoned to death by a mob because of his preaching. Here's the way the writer put it in Acts 7:59–60:

"They were stoning Stephen as he called out: 'Lord Jesus, receive my spirit!' Then he knelt down and cried out with a loud voice, 'Lord, do not charge them with this sin!' And saying this, he fell asleep."

Acts 13:36 takes this same concept and applies it to the Old Testament saints: "David, after serving his own generation in God's plan, fell asleep, was buried with his fathers, and decayed."

In a remarkable passage, the apostle Paul wrote to the Corinthians and told them to stop partaking of the Lord's Supper in a careless and casual manner. "This is why many are sick and ill among you," he said, "and many have fallen asleep" (1 Cor. 11:30).

Four chapters later, in the Resurrection Chapter—1 Corinthians 15—Paul wrote that after Jesus rose from the dead on Easter Sunday, He was seen by five hundred people, "most of whom remain to the present, but some have fallen asleep" (v. 6). Then he said in verse 20: "But now Christ has been raised from the dead, the firstfruits of those who have fallen asleep."

We have the same wording in 1 Thessalonians 4, where we're told not to be overly distressed about those who have fallen asleep, and not to grieve as those who have no hope.

This is Bible-speak. This is the way God sees it, and that's the way Christians throughout all the ages have viewed it. Our English word *cemetery* comes from the Greek word *koimaomai*, meaning "sleeping places" or "sleeping chambers."

The Bible doesn't teach that the soul goes to sleep. According to Scripture, when we die our soul goes to be with Jesus, and we're very awake and aware of things. Jesus said to the thief on the adjacent cross, "Today you will be with Me in paradise" (Luke 23:43b). The soul doesn't fall asleep, but the body does.

What, then, is the significance of the term *sleep*? Two things: The first is rest. When someone falls asleep, he or she is resting.

Revelation 14:13 says: "'Blessed are the dead who die in the Lord.' . . . 'Let them rest from their labors, for their works follow them!'"

The second implication is *rising*. Sleep is a temporary state. We fall asleep only to awaken in the morning. We die only to rise again. This same body will be reconstituted and resurrected at the last trumpet, and we shall rise again.

Jesus Is Our Loving Friend

There's another lesson for us in John 11: Jesus is our loving friend. I was amazed at how often this showed up in the text:

- Verse 3b: "'Lord, the one You love is sick.'"
- Verse 5: "Jesus loved Martha, her sister, and Lazarus."
- Verse 11b: "'Our friend Lazarus.'"
- Verse 36: "So the Jews said, 'See how He loved him!'"

Arriving at the tomb, Jesus was overcome with grief and wept by the graveside of His friend. I've pondered that quite a bit. Those tears were drops of liquid pain. Why did Jesus weep when He knew He was going to raise Lazarus to life?

To Him, I think, that graveyard scene was a microcosm of all the death and sorrow that strikes this earth 108 times each minute. I think Jesus felt the grief for every death that ever occurs, as represented by the tomb of that one man Lazarus. In so doing, Jesus was telling us that it's all right for us to weep, grieve, and sorrow when our dearest ones pass away. And He was telling us how much He loves us.

You can put your name in this very passage: See how Jesus loves you!

He loves us in life and in death, in the church and in the cemetery. I know this from personal experience, for when my father and, later, my mother passed away, I had a special word from the Lord Jesus on both occasions that comforted and sustained me. These were Bible verses that came suddenly and forcefully to mind. Jesus comes and speaks to us at our moments of grief exactly as He did to these two sisters.

Notice that Jesus wept, but He didn't wail. He sorrowed, but not as those who have no hope. He grieved but not excessively. In so doing, He set a pattern for us.

Samuel Willard (1640–1707) was a prominent New England Puritan who once delivered a funeral sermon upon the death of John Hull, America's first silversmith who became the wealthiest man in America in his day. Willard's sermon was titled "The Death of a Saint," and he had three points:

1. When the saints die let us mourn.
2. When the saints die beware of irregular mourning.
   Though we are to lament their death, yet we must beware that it be after the right manner. A dying saint may say to his weeping friends that stand round about, wringing their hands, after the same language that Christ did to those weeping women, "Daughters of Jerusalem, weep not for me, but for yourselves . . ." (Luke 23:27). We may therefore weep for ourselves, and there is good reason for it; but to mourn for them is superfluous. Is their death precious in God's (sight)? Let it not be miserable in our esteem: and tell me you whose hearts throb, and eyes run over with sorrow, is it not a precious thing to be asleep in Jesus? To lay in the lamp of His providence, and rest from the labors and sorrows of a troublesome world?
3. Is the death of the saints precious in God's sight? Let it be so in ours also.

One of the greatest preachers in the entire history of the church was John, the archbishop of Constantinople, who was called Chrysostom, which means "the golden mouth" because of the power of his sermons. He once preached a message on the subject "Excessive Grief at the Death of Friends," warning his audience that Jesus didn't want believers to sink down in hopeless, lonely, depressed, despondent despair when a believer went on to glory.

Neil and Carol Anderson served for many years as missionaries with Wycliffe Bible Translators in Papua New Guinea, and it was their great mission to bring the Word of God to a tribe of people who had never heard the gospel. One of the things that happened, of course, is that the new Christians changed the way they dealt with the subject of death. Carol told this story about a man in the village of Fukutao. His name was Erima, and he passed away while the Andersons were on a trip. They returned shortly after his death to find his widow sitting in front of the house, mourning. She looked a little haggard, but she was smiling. That was utterly amazing, because in that society when a man died, his widow was expected to sit by his graveside day and night, wailing and mourning, scarcely eating or sleeping.

She explained, "My husband died while you were gone, but he told me not to wail and mourn for him because he was going to God's place." Then she told them the entire story. Erima had been very sick, obviously dying. The family gathered around him very close, and finally the old man stopped breathing. The friends and family members, as the custom was, began wailing loudly, sobbing, crying, and mourning.

Suddenly to their great surprise, Erima opened his eyes. Instantly the wailing ceased, and everyone looked at the man in shock. Erima told them he had been to the Lord's place. He said it was brilliantly lighted and the surface of the ground was like a rainbow laid out flat. He told them not to mourn for him, and then he closed his eyes and died.

Now the family was faced with a great dilemma. In that culture, they were expected to engage in excessive, prolonged, and vociferous mourning. It was also the custom to burn the clothing of the deceased, kill his pigs, and destroy his garden, but Erima had returned to life, as it were, to tell them not to do that. So his widow, being a Christian, decided to obey her husband's advice. She grieved but not excessively. She didn't burn his clothes or destroy his pigs or crops. She did not put mud on her face and remain by his grave day after day.

It was the talk of the village. And it was a powerful witness that when Christ comes into a culture and into a home and into a heart, He changes the way believers view the process and the act of dying. We sorrow, but we sorrow not as those who have no hope.[1]

Jesus Is Our Resurrection Victory

The reason is because Jesus is our resurrection victory. Here in John 11, notice how this plays out in the conversation:

"'Your brother will rise again,' Jesus told her. Martha said, 'I know that he will rise again in the resurrection at the last day.' Jesus said to her, 'I am the resurrection and the life. The one who believes in Me, even if he dies, will live. Everyone who lives and believes in Me will never die—ever. Do you believe this?' 'Yes, Lord,' she told Him, 'I believe You are the Messiah, the Son of God, who was to come into the world'" (vv. 23–27).

Let's analyze this.

Jesus said, *"I am the resurrection."* Then He also said: *"I am the life."* There were two parts to the "I am" statements. It seems clear that each of them correspond to the two statements that follow:

---

1. Carol Anderson, "Going to God's Place," *JARRS Beyond*, vol. 28, num. 2, 6–7.

I am the Resurrection	I am the Life
Refers to the body	Refers to the soul
The one who believes in Me, even if he dies, will live.	Everyone who lives and believes in Me will never die.

In other words, Jesus said, in effect: "Now, as it relates to the human body of the believer, I am the resurrection. The person who believes in Me will live again, even if he dies. And as it relates to the soul, I am the life, and the person who lives and believes in Me will never actually die."

And then, in a mighty and massive demonstration of His power and authority, Jesus commanded the tombstone be rolled away. Looking upward to heaven, He offered a simple prayer, then gazed at the tomb and shouted: "Lazarus, come out!" (v. 43b).

The dead man came out bound hand and foot, and Jesus said, "Loose him and let him go" (v. 44b).

John 11 is a preview of what will happen around the world in a global instant when Jesus descends from heaven with a shout, as predicted in 1 Thessalonians 4. In that passage, Paul didn't disclose the nature of the shout, but John 11 leaves little doubt. I believe it will be the command, "Come forth!" The tombs will empty, and the dead in Christ will fly skyward like molecules of metal jerked upward by an irresistible magnet of mercy.

Rev. J. Reford Wilson was the director of my denomination's international missions department and a close friend. When his health began failing, he entered the hospital for a serious operation. The doctors warned him that his chances of survival were small. But, they said, surgery might help. Even so, the surgery itself contained risk, and his chances were marginal.

With his usual disarming, twinkling smile, Reford said, "Either way, Doc, I win."

As it turned out, Reford didn't make it through surgery, but it was all right. His sickness didn't end in death; it was for the glory of God.

Our Lord has the power and authority to reverse all the circumstances of both life and death, making all things work for our good—even in the cemetery. That's why Thomas Watson once said, "The world is but a great inn, where we are to stay a night or two, and be gone; what madness is it to set our heart upon our inn, as to forget our home. . . . A Christian's best things are to come."[2]

---

2. Thomas Watson, *Gleanings from Thomas Watson* (Morgan, PA: Soli Deo Gloria Publications, 1995), 115, 123.

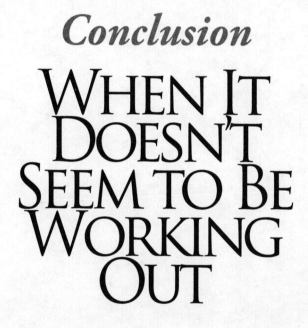

Conclusion

WHEN IT DOESN'T SEEM TO BE WORKING OUT

CHAPTER 18

All Things for Good, All Things for God

I f you're in the grips of pain or suffering right now, you might be asking, "What if it doesn't work? How can it possibly work? There's no way this will turn out for good. God has fallen asleep on the job, and nothing is working out at all."

Sometimes I'm caught in a vortex of depression and sadness that drains every ounce of happiness and hope out of my heart. Being melancholic by nature, very seldom do I feel perfectly and fully happy in terms of my emotions. We melancholics have to work at it all the time. Usually I manage well, but sometimes I feel the full weight of my problems and burdens.

That's how the writer of Psalm 44 felt. He penned his sentiments in a long poem that is breathtaking in its honesty. He begins by reciting the miracles God performed in earlier times as He led His people into the Promised Land and gave them victory after victory. As a result, they had worshiped Him with praises piled on praises.

God, we have heard with our ears—
our forefathers have told us—

the work You accomplished in their days,
in days long ago:
You give us victory over our foes. . . .
We boast in God all day long;
we will praise Your name forever. (vv. 1, 7–8)

Then in verse 9, the psalmist got to his primary point:

But You have rejected and humiliated us; . . .
You hand us over to be eaten like sheep
and scatter us among the nations.
You sell Your people for nothing; . . .
You make us a joke. (vv. 9a, 11–12a, 14a)

The psalmist felt abandoned by God, and worse, it was as if the Lord was deliberately rejecting the people. And it wasn't because they had sinned, said the writer in verses 17–21. There was no known spiritual reason for the sudden series of disastrous defeats suffered by God's people.

All this has happened to us,
but we have not forgotten You
or betrayed Your covenant.
Our hearts have not turned back. (vv. 17–18a)

Had the people sinned, explained the psalmist, he would understand why God was allowing these defeats and devastations.

If we had forgotten the name of our God
and spread out our hands to a foreign god,
wouldn't God have found this out,
since He knows the secrets of the heart? (vv. 20–21)

As far as the psalmist could see, these misfortunes and sorrows weren't coming as the result of sin or as punishment for disobedience. God was deliberately letting this happen to them. Verse 22 says bluntly,

> Because of You we are slain all day long;
> we are counted as sheep to be slaughtered.

Coming to the end of Psalm 44, the writer cried out,

> Wake up, LORD! Why are you sleeping? . . .
> For we have sunk down to the dust;
> our bodies cling to the ground.
> Rise up! Help us!
> Redeem us because of Your faithful love.
> (vv. 23a, 25–26)

Romans 8:28 is God's answer to the prayer of Psalm 44.

We know that because there's a direct link between the two passages. The apostle Paul, writing under the inspiration of the Holy Spirit, had been reading Psalm 44, and it was very much on his mind as he wrapped up Romans 8. Notice how Paul quoted from Psalm 44:22 in Romans 8.

Direct Link

Because of You we are slain all day long; we are counted as sheep to be slaughtered. (Ps. 44:22)	As it is written: "Because of You we are being put to death all day long; we are counted as sheep to be slaughtered." No, in all these things we are more than victorious through Him who loved us. (Rom. 8:36–37)

When we feel we're caught in Psalm 44, we need to pack our bags and relocate to Romans 8. We read Psalm 44 because it expresses our pain, and we read Romans 8 because it expresses God's promise to us. We have to talk to ourselves, pick ourselves up, preach to ourselves, and remind ourselves that God is faithful. He has the power to do what He has promised, and He will *do* as He has promised. Not one of His promises has ever failed. When we sing "Great Is Thy Faithfulness," that's exactly what we mean.

I'd like to close with an original hymn I've written based on the truth of the verses we've scanned in this book. It can be sung as it is on the next page or to any one of several existing hymn tunes.[1] Learn it, teach it to your children and to your church, and sing it as needed in your own life.

Or better yet, write your own song of praise. Find in the promises of Scripture the basis for all joy, all singing, and all optimism. Believe it! Everything that happens in our lives works out for the benefit of God-lovers.

We know that all things work together
for the good of those who love God:
those who are called according to His purpose.

---

1. DUNDEE (God moves in a mysterious way), WINCHESTER OLD, THIS ENDRIS NYGHT, ST. FLAVEN, ST. ANNE (O God our Help), ST. AGNES, HEREFORD (Ousley), GREENWICH, FINGAL, ST. STEVEN, ES KOMMT EN SCHEFF.

All Things for Good

Rob Morgan

Corey Hawkins

Praise God who works all things for good for
Though sin may harm and Sa - tan stalk, we
The world may mean it for our harm, but
Oh, that I might love Him su - preme and

those who love His name. His pro - vi - den - tial
can - not live in fear, for God who rules and
Christ is on His throne, His sov' - reign - ty works
trust Him in dis - tress; His pro - mis - es will

hand shall turn all bur - dens in - to gain.
o - ver rules com - mands: "Be of good cheer!"
for our good of those who are His own.
ne - ver fail, nor I His name to bless.

Sources of Epigraphs

Page xi: Charles Haddon Spurgeon, *Beside Still Waters,* Roy H. Clark, editor (Nashville: Thomas Nelson Publications, 1999), 243.

Page 15: Charles R. Erdman, *The Epistle of Paul to the Romans* (Philadelphia: Westminster Press, 1925), 102.

Page 31: David Martyn Lloyd-Jones, *Romans: The Final Perseverance of the Saints: Expositions of Chapters 8:17–39* (Grand Rapids, MI: Zondervan, 1975), 195.

Page 39: Quoted by Thomas Watson, *A Divine Cordial* (1663; repr., Lafayette, IN: Sovereign Grace, 2001), 36.

Page 51: Quoted by Mrs. Charles E. Cowman, *Springs in the Valley* (Los Angeles: Cowman Publications, 1939), 223.

Page 57: Watson, *A Divine Cordial,* 9.

Page 83: Thomas Watson, *Gleanings from Thomas Watson* (Morgan, PA: Soli Deo Gloria Publications, 1995), 141.

Page 107: R. C. Sproul, *The Invisible Hand* (Phillipsburg, NJ: P & R Publishing, 1996), 174.